vegie food

vegie
food

MURDOCH
B O O K S

Contents

Starters

Bruschetta

Classic Tuscan
6 ripe Roma (plum) tomatoes
15 g (½ cup) basil, shredded
1 garlic clove, finely chopped
2 tablespoons extra virgin olive oil

Mushroom and parsley
2 tablespoons olive oil
200 g (7 oz) small button mushrooms,
   quartered
1 tablespoon lemon juice
50 g (1¾ oz) goat's cheese, crumbled
1 tablespoon finely chopped flat-leaf
   (Italian) parsley
1 teaspoon chopped thyme

16 slices crusty white Italian-style
   bread, cut into 1 cm (½ inch) slices
4 garlic cloves, halved
60 ml (¼ cup) olive oil

To make the classic Tuscan topping, score a cross in the base of each tomato and place in a bowl of boiling water for 10 seconds, then plunge into cold water. Peel the skin away from the cross. Cut in half and scoop out the seeds with a teaspoon. Finely dice the flesh, then combine with the basil, garlic and oil.

To make the mushroom and parsley topping, heat the oil in a frying pan and cook the mushrooms over medium heat for 5 minutes, or until just tender. Remove from the heat and transfer to a small bowl. Stir in the lemon juice, goat's cheese, parsley and thyme.

Toast the bread and, while still hot, rub with the cut side of a garlic clove. Drizzle oil over each slice of bread, then season with salt and freshly ground black pepper. Divide the toppings among the bread slices.

Serves 8

Note: Each topping makes enough for eight slices of bruschetta. You will only need eight slices of bread if you only want to make one topping.

Chargrilled asparagus with salsa

3 eggs
2 tablespoons milk
1 tablespoon olive oil
2 corn cobs
1 small red onion, diced
1 red capsicum (pepper), finely
   chopped
2 tablespoons chopped thyme
2 tablespoons olive oil, extra
2 tablespoons balsamic vinegar
24 fresh asparagus spears
1 tablespoon macadamia oil
toasted wholegrain bread, to serve

Beat the eggs and milk to combine. Heat the oil in a non-stick frying pan over medium heat, add the egg and cook until just set. Flip and cook the other side. Remove and allow to cool, then roll up and cut into thin slices.

Cook the corn in a chargrill pan (griddle) or in boiling water until tender. Allow to cool slightly, then slice off the corn kernels. Make the salsa by gently combining the corn, onion, capsicum, thyme, extra olive oil and balsamic vinegar.

Trim off any woody ends from the asparagus spears, lightly brush with macadamia oil and cook in a chargrill pan (griddle) or on a barbecue hotplate until tender.

Serve the asparagus topped with a little salsa and the finely shredded egg, accompanied by fingers of buttered, toasted wholegrain bread.

Serves 4–6

Carrot timbales with creamy saffron and leek sauce

60 g (2¼ oz) butter
2 leeks, sliced
2 garlic cloves, crushed
1 kg (2 lb 4 oz) carrots, sliced
375 ml (1½ cups) vegetable stock
1½ tablespoons finely chopped sage
60 ml (¼ cup) cream
4 eggs, lightly beaten

Saffron and leek sauce
40 g (1½ oz) butter
1 small leek, finely sliced
1 large garlic clove, crushed
60 ml (¼ cup) white wine
pinch saffron threads
90 g (⅓ cup) crème fraîche

Preheat the oven to 170°C (325°F/ Gas 3). Lightly grease six 185 ml (¾ cup) timbale moulds. Heat the butter in a saucepan over medium heat, add the leek and cook for 3–4 minutes, or until soft. Add the garlic and carrot and cook for 2–3 minutes. Pour in the stock and 500 ml (2 cups) water, bring to the boil, then reduce the heat and simmer, covered, for 5 minutes, or until the carrot is tender. Strain, reserving 185 ml (¾ cup) of the liquid.

Blend the carrot, 125 ml (½ cup) of the reserved liquid and the sage until smooth. Cool slightly. Stir in the cream and egg, season and pour into the moulds. Place the moulds in a roasting tin filled with enough hot water to come halfway up their sides. Bake for 30–40 minutes, or until just set.

To make the sauce, melt the butter in a saucepan and cook the leek over medium heat for 3–4 minutes without browning. Add the garlic and cook for 30 seconds. Add the wine, remaining reserved liquid and saffron, and simmer for 5 minutes, or until reduced. Stir in the crème fraîche.

Invert the timbales onto serving plates and serve with the sauce.

Serves 6

Roasted field mushrooms with tarragon and lemon crème fraîche

80 ml (⅓ cup) olive oil
2 tablespoons lemon juice
4 garlic cloves, crushed
12 large flat field mushrooms,
    brushed and stems trimmed
2 tablespoons finely chopped
    flat-leaf (Italian) parsley
toasted bread, to serve

Lemon crème fraîche
60 ml (¼ cup) crème fraîche
2 teaspoons lemon juice
1 garlic clove, crushed
2 teaspoons chopped tarragon

Preheat the oven to 200°C (400°F/ Gas 6). In a large roasting tin, combine the oil, lemon juice and garlic. Add the mushrooms, and gently toss until coated. Season well with salt and pepper and arrange in a single layer. Roast for 30 minutes, turning to cook evenly.

Meanwhile, in a small bowl, combine the crème fraîche, lemon juice, garlic and tarragon.

Sprinkle the mushrooms and their cooking juices with parsley, and serve with the lemon crème fraîche and toasted bread.

Serves 4

Mini leek pies

60 g (2¼ oz) butter
2 tablespoons olive oil
1 onion, finely chopped
3 leeks, finely sliced
1 garlic clove, chopped
1 tablespoon plain (all-purpose)
  flour
2 tablespoons sour cream
100 g (1 cup) grated Parmesan
  cheese
1 teaspoon chopped thyme
4 sheets frozen puff pastry, thawed
1 egg, lightly beaten

Heat the butter and oil in a large frying pan over medium heat. Add the onion and cook, stirring occasionally, for 2 minutes. Add the leek and garlic and cook for 5 minutes, or until the leek is softened and lightly coloured. Add the flour and stir into the mixture for 1 minute. Add the sour cream and stir until slightly thickened. Transfer to a bowl and add the Parmesan and thyme. Season with salt and cracked black pepper and allow to cool.

Preheat the oven to 200°C (400°F/ Gas 6). Place a lightly greased baking tray in the oven to heat. Using a 6 cm (2½ inch) cutter, cut the pastry into 64 circles. Place 2 heaped teaspoons of filling on half the pastry circles, leaving a small border. Lightly brush the edges with egg, then place a pastry circle on top of each. Seal the edges well with a fork. Lightly brush the tops with egg.

Place the pies on the heated tray and bake for 25 minutes, or until the pies are puffed and golden.

Makes 32

Tempura vegetables with wasabi mayonnaise

Wasabi mayonnaise
2 tablespoons whole-egg mayonnaise
3 teaspoons wasabi paste
1/2 teaspoon grated lime zest

2 egg yolks
250 ml (1 cup) chilled soda water
30 g (1/4 cup) cornflour (cornstarch)
110 g (4 oz) plain (all-purpose) flour
40 g (1/4 cup) sesame seeds, toasted
oil, for deep-frying
1 small (250 g/9 oz) eggplant
  (aubergine), cut into thin rounds
1 large onion, cut into thin rounds,
  with rings intact
300 g (10½ oz) orange sweet potato,
  cut into thin rounds

To make the wasabi mayonnaise, combine all the ingredients. Transfer to a serving bowl, cover with plastic wrap and refrigerate.

Place the egg yolks and soda water in a jug and mix lightly with a whisk. Sift the cornflour and flour into a bowl. Add the sesame seeds and a good sprinkling of salt and mix well. Pour the soda water and egg yolk mixture into the flour and stir lightly with a fork or chopsticks until just combined but still lumpy.

Fill a deep heavy-based saucepan or wok one-third full of oil and heat until a cube of bread dropped into the oil browns in 15 seconds. Dip pairs of the vegetables — eggplant and onion or eggplant and sweet potato — into the batter and cook in batches for 3–4 minutes, or until golden brown and cooked through. Drain on crumpled paper towels; season well. Keep warm, but do not cover or the tempura coating will go soggy.

Transfer the tempura to a warmed serving platter and serve immediately with the wasabi mayonnaise.

Serves 4–6

Capsicum rolled with goat's cheese, basil and capers

4 large red capsicums (peppers)
5 g (¼ cup) flat-leaf (Italian) parsley, chopped
2 tablespoons chives, chopped
2 tablespoons baby capers, finely chopped
1 tablespoon balsamic vinegar
150 g (5½ oz) goat's cheese
16 basil leaves
olive oil, to cover
crusty Italian bread, to serve

Cut the capsicum into large flat pieces and remove any seeds. Place on a tray skin-side up under a hot grill (broiler) until the skin blisters and blackens. Place in a plastic bag and leave to cool, then peel away the skin. Cut into 3 cm (1¼ inch) wide pieces.

Combine the parsley, chives, capers and balsamic vinegar in a small bowl. Crumble in the goat's cheese, and mix well. Season with lots of pepper. Place a basil leaf on the inside of each capsicum piece, and top with a teaspoon of the goat's cheese mixture. Roll the capsicum over the goat's cheese and secure with a toothpick. Place in an airtight, non-reactive container and cover with olive oil. Refrigerate until required. Allow to return to room temperature before serving with crusty Italian bread.

Serves 4

Stuffed artichokes

40 g (¼ cup) raw almonds
4 young globe artichokes
150 g (5½ oz) fresh ricotta cheese
2 garlic cloves, crushed
80 g (1 cup) fresh coarse
  breadcrumbs
1 teaspoon finely grated lemon zest
50 g (½ cup) grated Parmesan
  cheese
7 g (¼ cup) chopped flat-leaf (Italian)
  parsley
1 tablespoon olive oil
2 tablespoons butter
2 tablespoons lemon juice

Preheat the oven to 180°C (350°F/ Gas 4). Spread the almonds on a baking tray and bake for 5–10 minutes, or until lightly golden. Keep a close watch, as the almonds will burn easily. Cool, remove from the tray and chop.

Remove any tough outer leaves from the artichokes. Cut across the artichokes, about 3 cm (1¼ inches) from the top, and trim the stalks, leaving about 2 cm (¾ inch). Rub with lemon and put in a bowl of cold water with a little lemon juice to prevent the artichokes from turning brown.

Combine the almonds, ricotta, garlic, breadcrumbs, lemon zest, Parmesan and parsley in a bowl and season. Gently separate the artichoke leaves and push the filling in between them. Place the artichokes carefully in a steamer and drizzle with the olive oil. Steam for 25–30 minutes, or until tender (test with a metal skewer). Remove and cook under a hot grill (broiler) for about 5 minutes to brown the filling.

Melt the butter in a saucepan, remove from the heat and stir in the lemon juice. Arrange the artichokes on a serving plate, drizzle with the butter sauce and season well.

Serves 4

Vegetable frittata with hummus and black olives

2 large red capsicums (peppers)
600 g (1 lb 5 oz) orange sweet
   potato, cut into 1 cm (½ inch)
   slices
60 ml (¼ cup) olive oil
2 leeks, finely sliced
2 garlic cloves, crushed
250 g (9 oz) zucchini (courgettes),
   thinly sliced
500 g (1 lb 2 oz) eggplant
   (aubergines), cut into 1 cm
   (½ inch) slices
8 eggs, lightly beaten
2 tablespoons finely chopped basil
125 g (1¼ cups) grated Parmesan
   cheese
200 g (7 oz) ready-made hummus
black olives, pitted and halved,
   to garnish

Cut the capsicums into large pieces, removing the seeds and membrane. Place, skin-side up, under a hot grill (broiler) until the skin blackens and blisters. Cool in a plastic bag. Peel.

Cook the sweet potato in a saucepan of boiling water for 4–5 minutes, or until just tender. Drain.

Heat 1 tablespoon of the oil in a deep round 23 cm (9 inch) frying pan and stir the leek and garlic over medium heat for 1 minute, or until soft. Add the zucchini and cook for 2 minutes, then remove from the pan.

Heat the remaining oil and cook the eggplant in batches for 2 minutes each side, or until golden. Line the base of the pan with half the eggplant, then the leek. Cover with the capsicum, remaining eggplant and sweet potato.

Combine the eggs, basil, Parmesan and some pepper. Pour the mixture over the vegetables. Cook over low heat for 15 minutes, or until almost cooked. Put the pan under a hot grill (broiler) for 2–3 minutes, or until golden and cooked. Cool, then invert onto a board. Cut into 30 squares. Top with hummus and half an olive.

Makes 30 pieces

Caramelized onion tartlets with feta and thyme

1 1/2 sheets ready-rolled shortcrust
  pastry
30 g (1 oz) unsalted butter
750 g (1 lb 10 oz) thinly sliced
  red onion
1 1/2 tablespoons soft brown sugar
1 1/2 tablespoons balsamic vinegar
1 teaspoon chopped thyme
100 g (3 1/2 oz) feta cheese
thyme sprigs, garnish

Preheat the oven to 180°C (350°F/
Gas 4). Using a 5 cm (2 inch) round
cutter, cut out 24 circles of pastry.
Place in lightly greased patty tins and
bake for 15 minutes, or until golden.

Meanwhile, melt the butter in a large
frying pan. Add the red onion and
cook over low heat for 35–40 minutes,
or until soft and golden. Add the
brown sugar, balsamic vinegar and
thyme. Season. Cook for another
10 minutes, then spoon into the
pastry shells.

Crumble the feta over the tartlets and
place under a hot grill (broiler) for
30 seconds, or until the cheese melts
slightly. Top with sprigs of thyme and
serve immediately.

Makes 24

Seasonal vegetable platter with saffron aïoli

Saffron aïoli
pinch saffron threads
2 egg yolks
3 garlic cloves, crushed
2 tablespoons lemon juice
315 ml (1¼ cups) canola oil

335 g (1 bunch) baby (dutch) carrots,
  scrubbed and trimmed, leaving
  2 cm (¾ inch) green stem
155 g (1 bunch) green asparagus,
  ends trimmed
100 g (3½ oz) baby corn
100 g (3½ oz) French beans, trimmed
2 witlof (chicory/Belgian endive),
  base trimmed and leaves separated
300 g (10½ oz) radishes, trimmed
  and washed well
sea salt, to serve
crusty bread, to serve

To make the aïoli, place the saffron in a small bowl with 1 tablespoon of water. Put the egg yolks into a food processor with the garlic and lemon juice and blend until smooth. With the motor running, start adding the canola oil, a few drops at a time until an emulsion forms, then add the remainder in a slow, steady stream until thick and fully combined. Slowly add 2 tablespoons of warm water to thin slightly, and season well with salt and white pepper. Spoon into a small bowl, and stir in the saffron water. Refrigerate until needed.

Blanch the carrots in boiling salted water for 3 minutes, then drain and refresh in cold water. (Or, if you like the crunch, serve them raw.) Blanch the asparagus in boiling salted water for 2 minutes until tender to the bite. Drain and refresh in cold water. Blanch the baby corn in boiling salted water for 1 minute, then drain and refresh. Blanch the French beans for 30 seconds in boiling salted water, drain and refresh.

Arrange all the vegetables on a serving platter with the saffron aïoli. Serve with sea salt and crusty bread.

Serves 4–6

Fresh rice paper rolls

Dipping sauce
60 ml (¼ cup) sweet chilli sauce
1 tablespoon lime juice

100 g (3½ oz) dried rice vermicelli
½ green mango, julienned
1 small Lebanese (short) cucumber,
  seeded and julienned
½ avocado, julienned
4 spring onions (scallions), thinly
  sliced
15 g (½ cup) coriander (cilantro)
  leaves
2 tablespoons chopped Vietnamese
  mint
1 tablespoon sweet chilli sauce
2 tablespoons lime juice
20 square (15 cm/6 inch) rice
  paper wrappers

To make the dipping sauce, mix together the chilli sauce and lime juice.

Place the vermicelli in a bowl, cover with boiling water and leave for 5 minutes, or until softened. Drain, then cut into short lengths.

Put the vermicelli, mango, cucumber, avocado, spring onion, coriander, mint, sweet chilli sauce and lime juice in a bowl and mix together well.

Working with no more than two rice paper wrappers at a time, dip each wrapper in a bowl of warm water for 10 seconds to soften, then lay out on a flat work surface. Put 1 tablespoon of the filling on the wrapper, fold in the sides and roll up tightly. Repeat with the remaining filling and rice paper wrappers. Serve immediately with the dipping sauce.

Makes 20

Note: Ensure the rice paper rolls are tightly rolled together or they will fall apart while you are eating them. These rolls can be made 2–3 hours ahead of time — layer the rolls in an airtight container between sheets of greaseproof paper or plastic wrap, then store in the refrigerator.

Asparagus gremolata

50 g (1¾ oz) butter
80 g (1 cup) coarse fresh white
 breadcrumbs
7 g (¼ cup) chopped flat-leaf
 (Italian) parsley
2 garlic cloves, very finely chopped
3 teaspoons very finely chopped
 lemon zest
400 g (14 oz) green asparagus,
 trimmed
1½ tablespoons virgin olive oil

Melt the butter in a heavy-based frying pan over high heat. Add the breadcrumbs and, using a wooden spoon, stir until the crumbs are golden and crisp. Remove to a plate to cool slightly.

Combine the parsley, garlic and lemon zest in a bowl, add the breadcrumbs, and season to taste with freshly ground black pepper.

Bring a large, wide saucepan of water to the boil, add the asparagus and cook for 2–3 minutes, or until just tender when pierced with a fine skewer. Drain well and arrange on a warmed serving plate. Drizzle with the olive oil and sprinkle gremolata over the top. Serve immediately.

Serves 4

Mushroom pâté with melba toast

50 g (1¾ oz) butter
1 small onion, chopped
3 garlic cloves, crushed
375 g (13 oz) button mushrooms,
  quartered
125 g (1 cup) slivered almonds,
  toasted
2 tablespoons cream
2 tablespoons finely chopped
  thyme
3 tablespoons finely chopped
  flat-leaf (Italian) parsley
6 thick slices wholegrain or
  wholemeal bread

Heat the butter in a large frying pan. Cook the onion and garlic over medium heat for 2 minutes, or until soft. Increase the heat, add the mushrooms and cook for 5 minutes, or until the mushrooms are soft and most of the liquid has evaporated. Leave to cool for 10 minutes.

Place the almonds in a food processor or blender and chop roughly. Add the mushroom mixture and process until smooth. With the motor running, gradually pour in the cream. Stir in the herbs and season with salt and cracked black pepper. Spoon into two 250 ml (1 cup) ramekins and smooth the surface. Cover and refrigerate for 4–5 hours to allow the flavours to develop.

To make the toast, preheat the oven to 180°C (350°F/Gas 4). Toast one side of the bread under a hot grill (broiler) until golden. Remove the crusts and cut each slice into four triangles. Place on a large oven tray in a single layer, toasted-side down, and cook for 5–10 minutes, or until crisp. Remove as they crisp. Spread with pâté and serve immediately.

Makes 24

Vegetable shapes with crème fraîche and fried leek

850 g (1 lb 14 oz) long thin
   orange sweet potatoes
5 beetroots
125 g (½ cup) crème fraîche
1 garlic clove, crushed
¼ teaspoon grated lime zest
oil, for deep-frying
2 leeks, cut lengthways into
   very fine slices

Bring two large saucepans of water to the boil over high heat and place the sweet potatoes in one and the beetroots in the other. Boil, covered, for 30–40 minutes, or until tender, adding more boiling water if it starts to evaporate. Drain separately and set aside until cool enough to touch. Remove the skins from the beetroots. Trim the ends from the beetroots and sweet potatoes and cut both into 1 cm (½ inch) slices. Using a biscuit cutter, cut the thin slices into shapes. Leave to drain on paper towels.

Place the crème fraîche, garlic and lime zest in a bowl and mix together well. Refrigerate until ready to use.

Fill a deep heavy-based saucepan one-third full of oil and heat until a cube of bread dropped into the oil browns in 10 seconds. Cook the leek in four batches for 30 seconds, or until golden brown and crisp. Drain well on crumpled paper towels and season with salt.

To assemble, place a teaspoon of the crème fraîche mixture on top of each vegetable shape and top with some fried leek.

Makes 35

Red capsicum and walnut dip with toasted pitta wedges

4 large red capsicums (peppers)
1 small red chilli
4 garlic cloves, in the skin
100 g (1 cup) walnuts, lightly
   toasted
50 g (1³/₄ oz) sourdough bread,
   crusts removed
2 tablespoons lemon juice
1 tablespoon pomegranate
   molasses
1 teaspoon ground cumin
pitta bread
olive oil
sea salt

Cut the capsicum into large flat pieces. Place on a tray skin-side up with the chilli and the whole garlic cloves, and cook under a hot grill (broiler) until the skin blackens and blisters. Transfer to a plastic bag and allow to cool. Gently peel away the capsicum and chilli skin, and remove the garlic skins.

Place the walnuts in a food processor and grind. Add the capsicum and chilli flesh, garlic, bread, lemon juice, pomegranate molasses and cumin, and blend until smooth. Stir in 2 tablespoons of warm water to even out the texture, and season well with salt. Cover and refrigerate overnight so the flavours develop.

Preheat the oven to 200°C (400°F/ Gas 6). Cut the pitta bread into wedges, brush with olive oil and lightly sprinkle with sea salt. Cook in the oven for about 5 minutes, or until golden brown. Allow to cool and become crisp.

Drizzle olive oil over the dip. Serve with the toasted pitta wedges.

Serves 6–8

Indonesian peanut fritters

Dipping sauce
1 tablespoon rice vinegar
1 tablespoon mirin
2 tablespoons kecap manis
1/4 teaspoon finely grated
   fresh ginger

175 g (1 cup) rice flour
1 garlic clove, crushed
1 teaspoon ground turmeric
1/2 teaspoon ground cumin
3 teaspoons sambal oelek
1 1/2 teaspoons ground coriander
1 tablespoon finely chopped
   coriander (cilantro) leaves
200 ml (7 fl oz) coconut milk
200 g (1 1/4 cups) roasted unsalted
   peanuts
oil, for deep-frying

To make the dipping sauce, combine all the ingredients and cover.

To make the peanut fritters, combine the flour, garlic, turmeric, cumin, sambal oelek, ground coriander, coriander leaves and 1/2 teaspoon salt in a bowl. Gradually add the coconut milk until the mixture is smooth. Stir in the peanuts and 50 ml (1 3/4 fl oz) hot water.

Fill a wok or deep heavy-based saucepan one-third full of oil and heat until a cube of bread dropped into the oil browns in 15 seconds. Cook level tablespoons of mixture in batches for 1–2 minutes, or until golden. Drain on paper towels and season well. Serve at once with the dipping sauce.

Makes 25

Roast pumpkin, feta and pine nut pastie

800 g (1 lb 12 oz) Jap pumpkin,
  skin removed and cut into 1 cm
  (½ inch) thick slices
2 tablespoons olive oil
3 garlic cloves, crushed
4 sheets butter puff pastry, cut into
  15 cm (6 inch) squares
100 g (3½ oz) marinated feta cheese
3 tablespoons oregano leaves,
  roughly chopped
2 tablespoons pine nuts, toasted
1 egg yolk
1 tablespoon milk
1 tablespoon sesame seeds
sea salt, to sprinkle

Preheat the oven to 220°C (425°F/ Gas 7). Place the pumpkin on a baking tray and toss with the olive oil, garlic and salt and pepper. Roast in the oven for 40 minutes, or until cooked and golden. Remove and allow to cool.

Evenly divide the pumpkin among the four pastry squares, placing it in the centre. Top with the feta, oregano and pine nuts. Drizzle with a little of the feta marinating oil. Bring two of the diagonally opposite corners together and pinch in the centre above the filling. Bring the other two diagonally opposite corners together, and pinch to seal along the edges. The base will be square, the top will form a pyramid. Twist the top to seal where all four corners meet.

Place the egg yolk and milk in a small bowl, and whisk with a fork to make an eggwash for the pastry.

Place the pasties on a greased baking tray and brush with the eggwash. Sprinkle with sesame seeds and sea salt and bake for 15 minutes, or until golden brown.

Serves 4

Vegetable dumplings

1 tablespoon oil
3 spring onions (scallions), sliced
2 garlic cloves, chopped
2 teaspoons grated fresh ginger
3 tablespoons chopped garlic chives
420 g (15 oz) choy sum, shredded
2 tablespoons sweet chilli sauce
3 tablespoons chopped coriander
  (cilantro) leaves
45 g (¼ cup) water chestnuts,
  drained and chopped
25 gow gee wrappers

Dipping sauce
½ teaspoon sesame oil
½ teaspoon peanut oil
1 tablespoon soy sauce
1 tablespoon lime juice
1 small red chilli, finely chopped

Heat the oil in a frying pan over medium heat and cook the spring onion, garlic, ginger and chives for 1–2 minutes, or until soft. Increase the heat to high, add the choy sum and cook for 4–5 minutes, or until wilted. Stir in the chilli sauce, coriander and water chestnuts. Allow to cool. If the mixture is too wet, squeeze dry.

Lay a wrapper on the work surface. Place a heaped teaspoon of the filling in the centre. Moisten the edge of the wrapper with water and pinch to seal, forming a ball. Trim. Repeat with the remaining wrappers and filling.

Half fill a wok with water and bring to the boil. Line a bamboo steamer with baking paper. Steam the dumplings, seam-side up, for 5–6 minutes.

To make the dipping sauce, combine all the ingredients. Serve with the dumplings.

Makes 25

Stuffed mushrooms

8 large cap mushrooms
40 g (1 ½ oz) butter
6 spring onions (scallions), chopped
3 garlic cloves, crushed
200 g (2 cups) day-old breadcrumbs
1 ½ tablespoons finely chopped
  oregano
2 tablespoons chopped flat-leaf
  (Italian) parsley
50 g (½ cup) grated Parmesan
  cheese
1 egg, lightly beaten
olive oil, for greasing and drizzling

Preheat the oven to 200°C (400°F/ Gas 6). Remove the stems from the mushrooms and discard. Wipe over the caps with a clean, damp cloth to remove any dirt.

Melt the butter in a small frying pan over medium heat, add the spring onion and cook for 2 minutes, or until soft. Add the crushed garlic and cook for another minute. Place the breadcrumbs in a bowl and pour in the spring onion mixture, then add the herbs, Parmesan and beaten egg. Season with salt and freshly cracked black pepper and mix together well.

Lightly grease a baking tray. Divide the stuffing evenly among the mushrooms, pressing down lightly. Arrange the mushrooms on the tray, drizzle with olive oil and bake in the oven for 15 minutes, or until the tops are golden and the mushrooms are cooked through and tender. Serve immediately.

Serves 8

Mini spinach pies

80 ml (1/3 cup) olive oil
2 onions, finely chopped
2 garlic cloves, chopped
150 g (5½ oz) small button
 mushrooms, roughly chopped
200 g (7 oz) English spinach,
 chopped
½ teaspoon chopped thyme
100 g (3½ oz) feta cheese, crumbled
750 g (1 lb 10 oz) home-made or
 bought shortcrust pastry
milk, to glaze

Heat 2 tablespoons of oil in a frying pan over medium heat and cook the onion and garlic for 5 minutes, or until soft and lightly coloured. Add the mushrooms and cook for 4 minutes, or until softened. Transfer to a bowl.

Heat 1 tablespoon of oil in the same pan over medium heat, add half the spinach and cook, stirring well, for 2–3 minutes, or until the spinach has softened. Add to the bowl with the onion. Repeat with the remaining oil and spinach. Add the thyme and feta to the bowl and mix. Season with salt and pepper and set aside to cool.

Preheat the oven to 200°C (400°F/ Gas 6) and grease two 12-hole round-based patty tins. Roll out half the pastry between two sheets of baking paper and cut out 24 rounds using a 7.5 cm (2¾ inch) cutter. Use these to line the patty tins, then divide the spinach mixture among the holes. Roll out the remaining pastry between the baking paper and cut out 24 rounds using a 7 cm (2¾ inch) cutter to top the pies. Cover the pies with the lids and press the edges with a fork to seal. Prick the tops once with a fork, brush with milk and bake for 15–20 minutes, or until golden.

Makes 24

Eggplant, tomato and goat's cheese stack

4 vine-ripened tomatoes
4 garlic cloves, chopped
1 tablespoon shredded basil
2 tablespoons finely chopped
    flat-leaf (Italian) parsley
60 ml (¼ cup) olive oil
1 large eggplant (aubergine),
    cut into 5 mm (¼ inch) slices
8 basil leaves (extra), torn
85 g (3 oz) goat's cheese, crumbled

Preheat the oven to 180°C (350°F/ Gas 4). Halve the tomatoes and scoop out the pulp. Sprinkle a quarter of the garlic into each tomato half, then top with the combined basil and parsley. Arrange the halves on a baking tray, drizzle with 1 tablespoon of oil, season to taste and bake for 40 minutes, or until soft.

Preheat the grill (broiler). Brush a baking sheet with olive oil, place the eggplant slices on the tray and brush with the remaining oil. Grill for 5 minutes, or until crisp and golden.

Lightly oil four 185 ml (¾ cup) ramekins. Line each with eggplant, then two basil leaves, 1 piece of tomato, some goat's cheese, another piece of tomato, then a final slice of eggplant. Bake for 20 minutes, then leave for 5 minutes before turning out.

Serves 4

Cauliflower fritters

600 g (1 lb 5 oz) cauliflower
55 g (½ cup) besan (chickpea flour)
2 teaspoons ground cumin
1 teaspoon ground coriander
1 teaspoon ground turmeric
pinch cayenne pepper
1 egg, lightly beaten
1 egg yolk
oil, for deep-frying

Cut the cauliflower into bite-sized florets. Sift the flour and spices into a bowl, then stir in ½ teaspoon salt.

Lightly whisk the beaten egg, egg yolk and 60 ml (¼ cup) water in a jug. Make a well in the centre of the dry ingredients and pour in the egg mixture, whisking until smooth. Stand for 30 minutes.

Fill a deep saucepan one-third full of oil and heat to 180°C (350°F), or until a cube of bread dropped into the oil browns in 15 seconds. Dip the florets into the batter, allowing the excess to drain into the bowl. Deep-fry in batches for 3–4 minutes per batch, or until puffed and browned. Drain, sprinkle with salt and extra cayenne, if desired, and serve hot.

Serves 4–6

Mini Thai spring rolls

Filling
80 g (3 oz) dried rice vermicelli
2 garlic cloves, crushed
1 carrot, grated
4 spring onions (scallions), finely
    chopped
1 tablespoon sweet chilli sauce
2 teaspoons grated fresh ginger
2 coriander (cilantro) roots, finely
    chopped
1½ tablespoons lime juice
1 teaspoon shaved palm sugar
2 tablespoons chopped coriander
    (cilantro) leaves
3 teaspoons sesame oil
1 tablespoon kecap manis

40 square (12.5 cm/5 inch)
    spring roll wrappers
oil, for deep-frying
sweet chilli sauce, to serve

To make the filling, soak the vermicelli in boiling water for 5 minutes. Drain and cut into short lengths. Mix with the remaining filling ingredients.

Working with one wrapper at a time, spoon 1 tablespoon of the filling onto one corner (on the diagonal), brush the edges with water and roll up diagonally, tucking in the edges as you go. Repeat with the remaining filling and wrappers.

Fill a wok or deep heavy-based saucepan one-third full of oil and heat until a cube of bread browns in 15 seconds. Cook in batches for 2–3 minutes, or until golden brown. Drain on paper towels. Serve with sweet chilli sauce.

Makes 40

Baked stuffed capsicums

2 red capsicums (peppers)
2 yellow capsicums (peppers)
2 teaspoons olive oil
16 basil leaves
2½ tablespoons capers in vinegar,
   drained, rinsed and chopped
3 tablespoons olive oil, extra
2 garlic cloves, crushed
3 teaspoons aged balsamic vinegar

Preheat the oven to 180°C (350°F/ Gas 4). Cut the capsicums in half lengthways, leaving the stem intact (or if they are very large, cut them into quarters). Scrape out the seeds and any excess pith. Drizzle the bottom of an ovenproof dish with the oil, and add the capsicums, skin-side down.

In each capsicum, place 2 basil leaves, then divide the chopped capers among them. Season well with salt and freshly ground pepper.

In a bowl, combine the extra oil with the garlic and balsamic vinegar, and drizzle evenly over the capsicums. Cover the dish with foil, and cook for 10–15 minutes, or until the capsicums have partially cooked.

Remove the foil, and cook for another 15–20 minutes, or until the capsicums are tender and golden on the edges. Serve warm or at room temperature.

Serves 4

Betel and tofu bites

2 tablespoons sugar
24 betel leaves or large basil leaves
1 tablespoon oil
2 garlic cloves, crushed
1 tablespoon grated fresh ginger
2 small red chillies, seeded and finely
  chopped
200 g (7 oz) fried tofu puffs, shredded
2 fresh kaffir (makrut) lime leaves,
  finely shredded
3 tablespoons lime juice
2 tablespoons shaved palm sugar
  or soft brown sugar
3 tablespoons coriander (cilantro)
  leaves
25 g (¼ cup) desiccated coconut,
  toasted

In a bowl, combine the sugar and
500 ml (2 cups) water. Stir in the
betel leaves, soak for 10 minutes,
then drain.

Heat the oil in a frying pan and
cook the garlic, ginger and chilli
over medium heat for 1 minute.
Add the tofu, lime leaves and the
combined lime juice, palm sugar
and coriander. Stir until the tofu is
heated through.

Put 1 tablespoon of the tofu mixture
onto each betel leaf and lightly
sprinkle with coconut. Roll up the
leaves tightly and serve.

Makes 24

Beetroot hummus

500 g (1 lb 2 oz) beetroot
80 ml (⅓ cup) olive oil
1 large onion, chopped
1 tablespoon ground cumin
400 g (14 oz) tin chickpeas,
   drained
1 tablespoon tahini
80 g (⅓ cup) plain yoghurt
3 garlic cloves, crushed
60 ml (¼ cup) lemon juice
125 ml (½ cup) vegetable stock
Lebanese or Turkish bread, to serve

Scrub the beetroot well. Bring a large saucepan of water to the boil over high heat and cook the beetroot for 35–40 minutes, or until soft and cooked through. Drain and cool slightly before peeling.

Meanwhile, heat 1 tablespoon of the oil in a frying pan over medium heat and cook the onion for 2–3 minutes, or until soft. Add the cumin and cook for a further 1 minute, or until fragrant.

Chop the beetroot and place in a food processor or blender with the onion mixture, chickpeas, tahini, yoghurt, garlic, lemon juice and stock, and process until smooth. With the motor running, add the remaining oil in a thin steady stream. Process until the mixture is thoroughly combined. Serve the hummus with Lebanese or Turkish bread.

Serves 8

Note: You can use 500 g (1 lb 2 oz) of any vegetable to make the hummus. Try carrot or pumpkin.

Stuffed zucchini flowers

75 g (2½ oz) plain (all-purpose) flour
100 g (3½ oz) mozzarella cheese
10 basil leaves, torn
20 zucchini (courgette) blossoms,
  stems and pistils removed
olive oil, for shallow-frying
2 lemon wedges, to serve

In a bowl, combine the flour with about 250 ml (1 cup) water, enough to obtain a creamy consistency. Add a pinch of salt and mix.

Cut the mozzarella cheese into 20 matchsticks. Insert a piece of mozzarella and some basil into each zucchini blossom. Gently press the petals closed.

Pour oil into a heavy-based frying pan to a depth of 2.5 cm (1 inch). Heat until a drop of batter sizzles when dropped in the oil.

Dip one flower at a time in the batter, shaking off the excess. Cook in batches for 3 minutes, or until crisp and golden. Drain on paper towels. Season and serve immediately with lemon wedges.

Makes 20

Vegetable pakoras with spiced yoghurt

Spiced yoghurt
1 teaspoon cumin seeds
200 g (7 oz) plain yoghurt
1 garlic clove, crushed
15 g (½ cup) coriander (cilantro)
  leaves, chopped

35 g (⅓ cup) besan (chickpea flour)
40 g (⅓ cup) self-raising flour
45 g (⅓ cup) soy flour
½ teaspoon ground turmeric
1 teaspoon cayenne pepper
½ teaspoon ground coriander
1 small green chilli, seeded and
  finely chopped
oil, for deep-frying
200 g (7 oz) cauliflower, cut into
  small florets
140 g (5 oz) orange sweet potato,
  cut into 5 mm (¼ inch) slices
180 g (6 oz) eggplant (aubergine),
  cut into 5 mm (¼ inch) slices
180 g (6 oz) fresh asparagus, cut
  into 6 cm (2½ inch) lengths

To make the spiced yoghurt, heat a small frying pan over medium heat. Add the cumin seeds and dry-fry for 1–2 minutes, or until aromatic (shake the pan frequently to prevent the seeds from burning). Transfer to a mortar and pestle or spice grinder and roughly grind. Whisk into the yoghurt with the garlic. Season with salt and freshly ground black pepper, then stir in the coriander.

Place the besan, self-raising and soy flours, turmeric, cayenne, ground coriander, chilli and 1 teaspoon salt in a bowl. Gradually whisk in 250 ml (1 cup) cold water to form a batter. Leave for 15 minutes. Preheat the oven to 120°C (250°F/Gas ½).

Fill a small saucepan one-third full of oil and heat until a cube of bread browns in 20 seconds. Dip the vegetables in the batter and deep-fry in small batches for 1–2 minutes, or until pale gold. Remove with a slotted spoon and drain well on paper towels. Keep warm in the oven until all the vegetables are cooked.

Serve the hot vegetable pakoras with the spiced yoghurt.

Serves 4

Individual Italian summer tarts

60 ml (¼ cup) olive oil
2 red onions, sliced
1 tablespoon balsamic vinegar
1 teaspoon soft brown sugar
1 tablespoon chopped thyme
1 sheet ready-rolled puff pastry
170 g (6 oz) jar marinated quartered
   artichokes, drained
16 black olives, pitted
extra virgin olive oil, to serve
thyme sprigs, to garnish

Heat 2 tablespoons of the oil in a saucepan over low heat. Add the onion and cook, stirring occasionally, for 15 minutes, or until soft. Add the vinegar and brown sugar and cook for 15 minutes, or until lightly browned. Remove from the heat, stir in the chopped thyme and set aside to cool.

Preheat the oven to 220°C (425°F/ Gas 7) and heat a lightly greased baking tray. Cut four 10 cm (4 inch) rounds from the sheet of puff pastry and spread the onion over them, leaving a 1.5 cm (⁵⁄₈ inch) border.

Place the pastry bases on the hot baking tray and cook in the top half of the oven for 12–15 minutes, or until the edges are risen and the pastry is golden brown.

Arrange the artichokes over the onion, then fill the spaces with olives. Drizzle the tarts with extra virgin olive oil and serve garnished with thyme.

Serves 4

Artichokes in aromatic vinaigrette

2 tablespoons lemon juice
4 large globe artichokes
2 garlic cloves, crushed
1 teaspoon finely chopped oregano
1/2 teaspoon ground cumin
1/2 teaspoon ground coriander
pinch dried chilli flakes
3 teaspoons sherry vinegar
60 ml (1/4 cup) olive oil

Add the lemon juice to a large bowl of cold water. Trim the artichokes, cutting off the stalks to within 5 cm (2 inches) of the base and removing the tough outer leaves. Cut the top quarter of the leaves from each. Slice each artichoke in half from top to base, or into quarters if large. Remove each small, furry choke with a teaspoon, then put the artichokes in the bowl of acidulated water to prevent them from discolouring while you prepare the rest.

Bring a large non-reactive saucepan of water to the boil, add the artichokes and a teaspoon of salt and simmer for 20 minutes, or until tender. The cooking time will depend on the artichoke size. Test by pressing a skewer into the base. If cooked, the artichoke will be soft and give little resistance. Strain, then place the artichokes on their cut side to drain.

Combine the garlic, oregano, cumin, coriander and chilli flakes in a bowl. Season, and blend in the vinegar. Beating constantly, slowly pour in the oil to form an emulsion. This can be done in a small food processor.

Arrange the artichokes in rows on a platter. Pour the vinaigrette over the top and leave to cool completely.

Serves 4

Spinach and leek fritters

40 g (1½ oz) butter
40 g (¼ cup) pine nuts
1 leek, white part only, thinly sliced
100 g (3½ oz) baby English spinach,
  chopped
3 eggs
1 egg yolk
1 tablespoon cream
75 g (¾ cup) grated Parmesan
  cheese
1 tablespoon chopped parsley
1 tablespoon olive oil

Melt half the butter in a heavy-based frying pan over low–medium heat and cook the pine nuts and leek for 3 minutes, or until the pine nuts are golden. Add the spinach and cook for 1 minute. Remove the mixture from the pan and allow to cool slightly. Wipe out the pan with paper towels.

Whisk the eggs, yolk and cream together in a large bowl. Add the cheese and parsley and season with salt and freshly ground black pepper. Stir in the spinach mixture.

Melt half of the remaining butter and half of the oil in the frying pan. Place four 5–7 cm (2–2¾ inch) egg rings in the pan, and pour 60 ml (¼ cup) of the spinach mixture into each. Cook over low heat for 2–3 minutes, or until the base is set. Gently flip and cook the other side for 2–3 minutes, or until firm. Transfer to a plate and slide out of the egg rings. Repeat with the remaining butter, oil and spinach mixture. Serve immediately.

Makes 8

Potato tortilla

500 g (1 lb 2 oz) potatoes, cut
  into 1 cm (½ inch) slices
60 ml (¼ cup) olive oil
1 brown onion, thinly sliced
4 garlic cloves, thinly sliced
2 tablespoons finely chopped
  flat-leaf (Italian) parsley
6 eggs

Place the potato slices in a large
saucepan, cover with cold water and
bring to the boil over high heat. Boil
for 5 minutes, then drain and set aside.

Heat the oil in a deep-sided non-stick
frying pan over medium heat. Add
the onion and garlic and cook for
5 minutes, or until the onion softens.

Add the potato and parsley to the
pan and stir to combine. Cook over
medium heat for 5 mintues, gently
pressing down into the pan.

Whisk the eggs with 1 teaspoon each
of salt and freshly ground pepper and
pour evenly over the potato. Cover
and cook over low–medium heat for
about 20 minutes, or until the egg is
just set. Slide onto a serving plate or
serve directly from the pan.

Serves 6–8

Udon noodle sushi rolls

300 g (10$^{1}/_{2}$ oz) flat udon or
  soba noodles
6 sheets roasted nori
50 g (1$^{3}/_{4}$ oz) pickled daikon, cut
  into long, thin strips
3 tablespoons drained red pickled
  ginger shreds
ponzu sauce, for dipping (see Note)

Cook the udon or soba noodles according to the packet instructions or until tender. Rinse under cold water and pat dry.

Working on a flat surface, lie one sheet of nori on a sushi mat. Top with one-sixth of the noodles along the bottom half of the nori, then arrange the daikon and the pickled ginger along the centre of the noodles. Roll the nori up firmly to enclose the filling. Cut the roll in half and then each half into three equal pieces. Repeat with the remaining ingredients. Serve with the ponzu sauce.

Makes 36 pieces

Note: Ponzu is a Japanese dipping sauce made from rice vinegar, soy, mirin and dashi.

Individual vegetable terrines with spicy tomato sauce

125 ml (½ cup) oil
2 zucchini (courgettes), sliced
  on the diagonal
500 g (1 lb 2 oz) eggplant
  (aubergines), sliced
1 small fennel bulb, sliced
1 red onion, sliced
300 g (10½ oz) ricotta cheese
50 g (½ cup) grated Parmesan
  cheese
1 tablespoon chopped flat-leaf
  (Italian) parsley
1 tablespoon chopped chives
1 red and 1 yellow capsicum (pepper),
  grilled (broiled), peeled, cut into
  large pieces

Spicy tomato sauce
1 tablespoon oil
1 onion, finely chopped
2 garlic cloves, crushed
1 red chilli, seeded and chopped
425 g (15 oz) tin chopped tomatoes
2 tablespoons tomato paste (purée)

Heat 1 tablespoon of the oil in a large frying pan over high heat. Cook the zucchini, eggplant, fennel and onion in batches for 5 minutes, or until golden, adding oil as needed. Drain separately on paper towels.

Preheat the oven to 200°C (400°F/ Gas 6). Mix together the ricotta, Parmesan, parsley and chives. Season well.

Lightly grease and line four 315 ml (1¼ cup) ramekins. Using half the eggplant, line the base of each dish. Continue layering with the zucchini, capsicum, cheese mixture, fennel and onion. Cover with the remaining eggplant and press down firmly. Bake for 10–15 minutes, or until hot. Leave for 5 minutes before turning out.

Meanwhile, to make the sauce, heat the oil in a saucepan and cook the onion and garlic for 2–3 minutes, or until soft. Add the chilli, chopped tomato and tomato paste and simmer for 5 minutes, or until thick and pulpy. Purée in a food processor. Return to the saucepan and keep warm. Spoon over the terrines.

Serves 4

Soups

Jerusalem artichoke and roast garlic soup

1 garlic head
2 tablespoons butter
1 tablespoon olive oil
1 onion, chopped
1 leek, white part only, washed
 and chopped
1 celery stalk, chopped
700 g (1 lb 9 oz) Jerusalem
 artichokes, peeled and chopped
1 small potato, chopped
1.5 litres (6 cups) vegetable or
 chicken stock
olive oil, to serve
finely chopped chives, to serve

Preheat the oven to 200°C (400°F/
Gas 6). Slice the base from the head
of garlic, wrap it in foil and roast for
30 minutes, or until soft. When cool
enough to handle, remove from the
foil and slip the cloves from the skin.
Set aside.

In a large heavy-based saucepan,
heat the butter and oil. Add the onion,
leek and celery and a large pinch of
salt, and cook for 10 minutes, or until
soft. Add the Jerusalem artichokes,
potato and garlic and cook for a
further 10 minutes. Pour in the stock,
bring the mixture to the boil, then
reduce the heat and simmer for
30 minutes, or until the vegetables
are soft.

Purée in a blender until smooth, and
season well. Serve with a drizzle of
olive oil and some chives. Delicious
with warm crusty bread.

Serves 4

Miso soup with udon and tofu

1 teaspoon dashi granules
3 tablespoons red (genmai) miso
2 tablespoons soy sauce
400 g (14 oz) fresh udon noodles,
  separated
400 g (14 oz) silken firm tofu, cubed
100 g (3½ oz) fresh shiitake
  mushrooms, sliced
500 g (1 bunch) baby bok choy
  (pak choi), leaves separated

Place the dashi, miso, soy sauce and 1.25 litres (5 cups) water in a large saucepan and bring to the boil. Reduce the heat and simmer for 10 minutes.

Add the udon noodles and cook for 5 minutes, or until soft. Stir in the tofu, shiitake mushrooms and bok choy and cook for 3 minutes, or until the bok choy wilts.

Serves 2–4

Green soup with pistou

60 ml (¼ cup) olive oil
1 onion, finely chopped
2 garlic cloves, crushed
1 celery stalk, chopped
1 zucchini (courgette), cut into
  1 cm (½ inch) rounds
1 head broccoli, cut into 1 cm
  (½ inch) pieces
1.5 litres (6 cups) vegetable or
  chicken stock
150 g (5½ oz) green beans, trimmed
  and cut into 1 cm (½ inch) pieces
155 g (1 cup) green peas
155 g (1 bunch) asparagus,
  end trimmed and cut into
  1 cm (½ inch) pieces
80 g (2 cups) shredded silverbeet
  (Swiss chard) leaves

Pistou
3 garlic cloves, peeled
20 g (⅔ cup) basil
80 ml (⅓ cup) olive oil
50 g (½ cup) grated Parmesan
  cheese

Heat the olive oil in a large saucepan, and cook the onion, garlic and celery until golden. Add the zucchini and broccoli, and cook for 5 minutes.

Add the stock and bring to the boil. Simmer for 5 minutes, then add the green beans, peas, asparagus and silverbeet. Simmer for 5 minutes, or until the vegetables are tender. Season well with salt and pepper.

To make the pistou, place the garlic and basil in a mortar and pestle or small food processor and crush together. Slowly add the oil, and blend until a smooth paste. Stir in the Parmesan, and season well with salt and pepper.

Ladle the soup into bowls and serve with a dollop of pistou.

Serves 4

Borscht
(cold beetroot soup)

6 large (1.5 kg/3 lb 5 oz) beetroot,
  peeled
1 1/2 tablespoons caster (superfine)
  sugar
125 ml (1/2 cup) lemon juice
3 eggs
sour cream, to serve (optional)

Grate the beetroot, and place in a
saucepan with the caster sugar and
2.25 litres (9 cups) water. Stir over low
heat until the sugar has dissolved.
Simmer, partially covered, for about
30 minutes, skimming the surface
occasionally.

Add the lemon juice and simmer,
uncovered, for 10 minutes. Remove
the pan from the heat.

Whisk the eggs in a bowl. Gradually
pour the eggs into the beetroot
mixture, whisking constantly and
taking care not to curdle the eggs.
Season to taste with salt and pepper.
Allow the soup to cool, then cover
and refrigerate until cold. Delicious
served with a dollop of sour cream.

Serves 6

Gazpacho

1 kg (2 lb 4 oz) vine-ripened
  tomatoes, chopped
1 Lebanese (short) cucumber,
  chopped
1 small red capsicum (pepper),
  seeded and chopped
1 red onion, chopped
3 garlic cloves
80 g (3 oz) sourdough bread,
  crusts removed
2 tablespoons sherry vinegar
Tabasco sauce

Dressing
2 teaspoons each of finely diced
  tomato, red capsicum (pepper),
  red onion, Lebanese (short)
  cucumber
2 teaspoons finely chopped
  flat-leaf (Italian) parsley
1 tablespoon extra virgin olive oil
1 teaspoon lemon juice

In a blender, place the tomatoes, cucumber, capsicum, onion, garlic, sourdough and 250 ml (1 cup) cold water, and blend until smooth. Pass through a strainer into a bowl, and add the sherry vinegar. Season to taste with salt and Tabasco, then cover and refrigerate for at least 2 hours or overnight to allow the flavours to develop.

To make the dressing, combine all the ingredients in a small bowl. Season.

Stir the gaspacho well, then ladle into bowls. Spoon the dressing over the top before serving.

Serves 4

Vegetable soup

105 g (½ cup) dried red kidney
   beans or borlotti beans
1 tablespoon olive oil
1 leek, halved lengthways and
   chopped
1 small onion, diced
2 carrots, chopped
2 celery stalks, chopped
1 large zucchini (courgette), chopped
1 tablespoon tomato paste (purée)
1 litre (4 cups) vegetable stock
400 g (14 oz) butternut pumpkin
   (squash), cut into 2 cm (¾ inch)
   cubes
2 potatoes, cut into 2 cm (¾ inch)
   cubes
3 tablespoons chopped flat-leaf
   (Italian) parsley

Place the beans in a large bowl, cover with cold water and soak overnight. Rinse, then transfer to a saucepan, cover with cold water and cook for 45 minutes, or until just tender. Drain.

Heat the olive oil in a saucepan. Add the leek and onion and cook over medium heat for 2–3 minutes without browning, until they start to soften. Add the carrot, celery and zucchini and cook for 3–4 minutes. Add the tomato paste and stir for 1 minute. Pour in the vegetable stock and 1.25 litres (5 cups) water and bring to the boil. Reduce the heat to low and simmer for 20 minutes.

Add the pumpkin, potato, parsley and beans and simmer for a further 20 minutes, or until the vegetables are tender and the beans are cooked. Season well. Serve with crusty bread.

Serves 6

Laksa

200 g (7 oz) dried rice vermicelli
2 tablespoons peanut oil
2–3 tablespoons laksa paste
1 litre (4 cups) vegetable stock
750 ml (3 cups) coconut milk
250 g (9 oz) snowpeas (mangetout),
    halved diagonally
5 spring onions (scallions), cut into
    3 cm (1¼ inch) lengths
2 tablespoons lime juice
125 g (4½ oz) bean sprouts
200 g (7 oz) fried tofu puffs, halved
3 tablespoons roughly chopped
    Vietnamese mint
20 g (⅔ cup) coriander (cilantro)
    leaves

Place the vermicelli in a large bowl,
cover with boiling water and soak
for 5 minutes.

Heat the oil in a large saucepan, add
the laksa paste and cook, stirring,
over medium heat for 1 minute, or
until fragrant. Add the stock, coconut
milk, snowpeas and spring onion and
simmer for 5 minutes. Pour in the lime
juice and season to taste with salt
and freshly ground black pepper.

Drain the vermicelli and divide among
four bowls. Top with the bean sprouts
and fried tofu puffs. Ladle the hot
soup into the bowls and sprinkle
with the fresh mint and coriander.
Serve immediately.

Serves 4

Asparagus soup

750 g (1 lb 10 oz) fresh asparagus
 spears
1 litre (4 cups) vegetable or
 chicken stock
30 g (1 oz) butter
1 tablespoon plain (all-purpose)
 flour
½ teaspoon finely grated
 lemon zest
extra lemon zest, to garnish

Trim and discard any woody ends from the asparagus spears and cut into 2 cm (¾ inch) lengths. Place in a large saucepan and add 500 ml (2 cups) of the stock. Cover and bring to the boil, then cook for 10 minutes, or until the asparagus is tender.

Transfer the asparagus and the hot stock to a blender or food processor, and purée in batches until smooth. Melt the butter in the saucepan over low heat, add the flour, then cook, stirring, for about 1 minute, or until pale and foaming. Remove from the heat and gradually add the remaining stock, stirring until smooth after each addition. When all the stock has been added, return the saucepan to the heat, bring to the boil, then simmer for 2 minutes.

Add the asparagus purée to the pan and stir until combined. When heated through, stir in the lemon zest and season with salt and cracked black pepper. Garnish with the lemon zest.

Serves 4

Chilli, corn and red capsicum soup

1 coriander (cilantro) sprig
4 cobs sweet corn
30 g (1 oz) butter
2 red capsicums (peppers), diced
1 small onion, finely chopped
1 small red chilli, finely chopped
1 tablespoon plain (all-purpose) flour
500 ml (2 cups) vegetable stock
125 ml (½ cup) cream

Trim the leaves off the coriander and finely chop the root and stems. Cut the kernels off the corn cobs.

Heat the butter in a saucepan over medium heat. Add the corn kernels, capsicum, onion and chilli and stir to coat in the butter. Cook, covered, over low heat, stirring occasionally, for 10 minutes, or until soft. Increase the heat to medium, add the coriander root and stem and cook, stirring, for 30 seconds, or until fragrant. Sprinkle with the flour and stir for 1 minute. Remove from the heat and gradually stir in the stock. Add 500 ml (2 cups) water and return to the heat. Bring to the boil, reduce the heat to low and simmer, covered, for 30 minutes, or until the vegetables are tender. Cool slightly.

Ladle 500 ml (2 cups) of the soup into a blender and purée until smooth. Return the purée to the soup in the pan, pour in the cream and gently heat until warmed through. Season. Sprinkle with the coriander leaves and serve. Delicious with grilled cheese on pitta bread.

Serves 4

Soba noodle and vegetable soup

250 g (9 oz) soba noodles
2 dried shiitake mushrooms
2 litres (8 cups) vegetable stock
120 g (4 oz) snowpeas (mangetout),
    cut into strips
2 small carrots, cut into thin 5 cm
    (2 inch) strips
2 garlic cloves, finely chopped
6 spring onions (scallions), cut into
    5 cm (2 inch) lengths and thinly
    sliced lengthways
3 cm (1 ¼ inch) piece ginger, cut
    into julienne strips
80 ml (⅓ cup) soy sauce
60 ml (¼ cup) mirin or sake
90 g (1 cup) bean sprouts
coriander (cilantro) leaves, to garnish

Cook the noodles according to the packet instructions. Drain.

Soak the mushrooms in 125 ml (½ cup) boiling water until soft. Drain, reserving the liquid. Remove the stalk and slice the mushrooms.

Combine the stock, mushrooms, reserved liquid, snowpeas, carrot, garlic, spring onion and ginger in a large saucepan. Bring slowly to the boil, then reduce the heat to low and simmer for 5 minutes, or until the vegetables are tender. Add the soy sauce, mirin and bean sprouts. Cook for a further 3 minutes.

Divide the noodles among four large serving bowls. Ladle the hot liquid and vegetables over the top and garnish with coriander.

Serves 4

Pumpkin and red lentil soup

1 tablespoon olive oil
1 long red chilli, seeded and
  chopped
1 onion, finely chopped
500 g (1 lb 2 oz) butternut pumpkin
  (squash), chopped
350 g (12 oz) orange sweet potato,
  chopped
1.5 litres (6 cups) vegetable stock
125 g (½ cup) red lentils
1 tablespoon tahini
red chilli, extra, to garnish

Heat the oil in a large saucepan over medium heat, add the chilli and onion and cook for 2–3 minutes, or until the onion is soft. Reduce the heat to low, add the pumpkin and sweet potato and cook, covered, for 8 minutes, stirring occasionally.

Increase the heat to high, add the stock and bring to the boil. Reduce the heat to low, and simmer, covered, for 10 minutes. Add the red lentils and cook, covered, for 7 minutes, or until tender.

Process the soup in batches in a blender or food processor, add the tahini and blend until smooth. Return to the saucepan and gently heat until warmed through. Garnish with chilli.

Serves 4

Carrot and ginger soup

750 ml (3 cups) vegetable stock
1 tablespoon oil
1 onion, chopped
1 tablespoon grated fresh ginger
1 kg (2 lb 4 oz) carrots, chopped
2 tablespoons chopped coriander
  (cilantro) leaves

Place the stock in a pan and bring to the boil. Heat the oil in a large heavy-based pan, add the onion and ginger and cook for 2 minutes, or until the onion has softened.

Add the stock and carrots. Bring to the boil, then reduce the heat and simmer for 10–15 minutes, or until the carrot is cooked and tender.

Place in a blender or food processor and process in batches until smooth. Return to the pan and add a little more stock or water to thin the soup to your preferred consistency.

Stir in the coriander and season to taste. Heat gently before serving.

Serves 4

Thai spicy sour soup

750 ml (3 cups) vegetable stock
2 tablespoons Tom Yum paste
(see Note)
2 cm x 2 cm (3/4 inch x 3/4 inch)
piece galangal, peeled and cut
into thin slices
1 stem lemon grass, lightly crushed
and cut into 4 lengths
3 fresh kaffir (makrut) lime leaves
1 small red chilli, finely sliced on
the diagonal (optional)
200 g (7 oz) button mushrooms,
halved
200 g (7 oz) silken firm tofu, cut
into 1.5 cm (5/8 inch) cubes
200 g (7 oz) baby bok choy
(pak choi), roughly shredded
2 tablespoons lime juice
4 tablespoons coriander (cilantro)
leaves

Place the stock, Tom Yum paste,
galangal, lemon grass, kaffir lime
leaves, chilli and 750 ml (3 cups)
water in a saucepan. Cover and
bring to the boil, then reduce the
heat and simmer for 5 minutes.

Add the mushrooms and tofu and
simmer for 5 minutes, or until the
mushrooms are tender. Add the
bok choy and simmer for a further
minute, or until wilted. Remove the
pan from the heat and stir in the
lime juice and coriander leaves
before serving.

Serves 4–6

Note: For vegetarian cooking, make
sure you buy a brand of Tom Yum
paste that does not contain shrimp
paste or fish sauce.

Silverbeet and risoni soup with Gruyère croutons

30 g (1 oz) butter
1 large onion, finely chopped
1 garlic clove, crushed
2 litres (8 cups) vegetable or
  chicken stock
200 g (1 cup) risoni
½ baguette, cut into 6 slices
15 g (½ oz) butter, extra, melted
1 teaspoon Dijon mustard
50 g (1¾ oz) Gruyère cheese,
  coarsely grated
500 g (1 lb 2 oz) silverbeet (Swiss
  chard), central stalk removed,
  shredded
30 g (1 cup) basil, torn

Heat the butter in a large heavy-based saucepan, add the onion and garlic and cook over medium heat for 2–3 minutes, or until the onion is softened. Meanwhile, place the stock in a separate pan and bring to the boil.

Add the stock to the onion mixture and bring to the boil. Add the risoni, reduce the heat and simmer for 8 minutes, stirring occasionally.

Meanwhile, place the baguette slices in a single layer on a baking tray and cook under a preheated grill (broiler) until golden brown on one side. Turn the slices over and brush with the combined melted butter and mustard. Top with the Gruyère and grill until the cheese has melted.

Add the silverbeet and basil to the risoni mixture and simmer for about 1 minute, or until the risoni is *al dente* and the silverbeet is cooked. Season with salt and freshly ground black pepper and serve with the Gruyère croutons.

Serves 6

Potato and sweet corn chowder

6 cobs sweet corn
2 tablespoons vegetable oil
1 onion, finely diced
3 garlic cloves, crushed
1 celery stalk, diced
1 carrot, peeled and diced
2 large potatoes, peeled and diced
1 litre (4 cups) vegetable or chicken
  stock
2 tablespoons finely chopped
  flat-leaf (Italian) parsley

Bring a large pot of salted water to the boil, and cook the sweet corn for 5 minutes. Reserve 250 ml (1 cup) of the cooking water. Cut the corn kernels from the cob, place half in a blender with the reserved cooking water, and blend until smooth.

Heat the oil in a large saucepan, add the onion, garlic, celery and a large pinch of salt and cook for 5 minutes. Add the carrot and potatoes, cook for a further 5 minutes, then add the stock, corn kernels and blended corn mixture. Reduce the heat and simmer for 20 minutes, or until the vegetables are tender. Season well, and stir in the chopped parsley before serving.

Serves 6

Curried lentil, carrot and cashew soup

1.5 litres (6 cups) vegetable or
  chicken stock
750 g (1 lb 10 oz) carrots, grated
185 g (³/₄ cup) red lentils, rinsed
  and drained
1 tablespoon olive oil
1 large onion, chopped
80 g (½ cup) unsalted cashew nuts
1 tablespoon Madras curry paste
25 g (½ cup) chopped coriander
  (cilantro) leaves and stems
125 g (½ cup) Greek-style yoghurt
coriander (cilantro) leaves, to garnish

Bring the stock to the boil in a large saucepan. Add the carrots and lentils, bring the mixture back to the boil, then simmer over low heat for about 8 minutes, or until the carrot and lentils are soft.

Meanwhile, heat the oil in a pan, add the onion and cashews and cook over medium heat for 2–3 minutes, or until the onion is soft and browned. Add the curry paste and coriander and cook for a further 1 minute, or until fragrant. Stir the paste into the carrot and lentil mixture.

Transfer to a food processor or blender and process in batches until smooth. Return the mixture to the pan and reheat over medium heat until hot. Season to taste with salt and cracked black pepper and serve with a dollop of yoghurt and a sprinkling of coriander.

Serves 6

Note: Garnish the soup with a pinch of chilli flakes to give it an extra kick.

Spicy parsnip soup

1.25 litres (5 cups) vegetable or
  chicken stock
30 g (1 oz) butter
1 white onion, cut into quarters
  and finely sliced
1 leek, finely sliced
500 g (1 lb 2 oz) parsnips, peeled
  and finely sliced
1 tablespoon Madras curry powder
1 teaspoon ground cumin
315 ml (1¼ cups) cream
10 g (⅓ cup) coriander (cilantro)
  leaves

Bring the stock to the boil in a saucepan and keep at a low simmer.

Place the butter in a large saucepan and melt over medium heat. Add the onion, leek and parsnip and cook, covered, for 5 minutes. Add the curry powder and cumin and cook for 1 minute. Stir in the stock and cook, covered, over medium heat for about 10 minutes, or until tender.

Transfer the soup to a blender or food processor and blend in batches until smooth. Return to the pan. Stir in the cream and warm through over low heat. Season to taste with salt and cracked black pepper and scatter with coriander leaves.

Serves 6

Note: This soup is also delicious without the cream.

Tomato and pasta soup

1.25 litres (5 cups) vegetable
   or chicken stock
90 g (1 cup) spiral pasta
2 carrots, sliced
1 zucchini (courgette), sliced
4 ripe tomatoes, roughly chopped
2 tablespoons shredded basil
fresh wholemeal loaf, to serve

Place the stock in a heavy-based saucepan and bring to the boil. Reduce the heat, add the pasta, carrot and zucchini and cook for about 5–10 minutes, or until the pasta is *al dente*.

Add the tomato and heat through gently for a few more minutes. Season to taste.

Pour the soup into warm soup bowls and sprinkle the basil over the top. Serve with a fresh wholemeal loaf.

Serves 4

Variation: To give this soup a slightly different flavour, serve with a dollop of fresh pesto.

Green curry vegetable soup

2 teaspoons peanut oil
1 tablespoon green curry paste
3 makrut (kaffir) lime leaves
1.25 litres (5 cups) vegetable or
  chicken stock
670 ml (2²/₃ cups) coconut milk
600 g (1 lb 5 oz) butternut pumpkin
  (squash), cut into 1.5 cm
  (⁵/₈ inch) cubes
250 g (9 oz) small yellow squash
  (pattypan squash), sliced
115 g (4 oz) fresh baby corn spears,
  halved lengthways
2 tablespoons mushroom soy sauce
2 tablespoons lime juice
1 teaspoon sugar
1½ tablespoons Vietnamese mint,
  finely chopped

Heat the oil in a large saucepan and add the curry paste and lime leaves. Cook, stirring, over medium heat for 1 minute, or until the mixture is fragrant. Bring the stock to the boil in a separate saucepan.

Gradually add the stock and coconut milk to the curry mixture and bring to the boil. Add the pumpkin, squash and corn, and simmer over low heat for 12 minutes, or until the pumpkin is tender.

Add the soy sauce and lime juice, and season to taste with sugar, salt and black pepper. Sprinkle with the mint before serving.

Serves 6

Sweet potato and pear soup

25 g (1 oz) butter
1 small white onion, finely chopped
750 g (1 lb 10 oz) orange sweet
    potato, peeled and cut into 2 cm
    ($3/4$ inch) dice
2 firm pears (500 g/1 lb 2 oz),
    peeled, cored and cut into 2 cm
    ($3/4$ inch) dice
750 ml (3 cups) vegetable or
    chicken stock
250 ml (1 cup) cream
mint leaves, to garnish

Melt the butter in a saucepan over medium heat, add the onion and cook for 2–3 minutes, or until softened but not brown. Add the sweet potato and pear, and cook, stirring, for 1–2 minutes. Add the stock to the pan, bring to the boil and cook for 20 minutes, or until the sweet potato and pear are soft.

Cool slightly, then place the mixture in a blender or food processor and blend in batches until smooth. Return to the pan, stir in the cream and gently reheat without boiling. Season with salt and ground black pepper. Garnish with the mint.

Serves 4

Mushroom and tortellini soup

1 tablespoon olive oil
175 g (6 oz) small flat mushrooms, sliced
6 spring onions (scallions), sliced
1 small garlic clove, crushed
1.25 litres (5 cups) vegetable or chicken stock
1 tablespoon port
2 teaspoons Worcestershire sauce
200 g (7 oz) fresh large ricotta tortellini
shaved Parmesan cheese, to garnish

Heat the oil in a large heavy-based saucepan. Add the mushrooms and cook over high heat for 2 minutes, browning the mushrooms before turning. Add the spring onion and garlic and cook for a further 1 minute.

Meanwhile, bring the stock to the boil in a separate saucepan. Add the stock, port and Worcestershire sauce to the mushroom mixture and bring to the boil. Add the tortellini and simmer for 8 minutes, or until the tortellini is *al dente*.

Season the soup with salt and cracked black pepper to taste and serve topped with shaved Parmesan.

Serves 4

Spring vegetable soup with basil pesto

1.25 litres (5 cups) vegetable or
  chicken stock
1 tablespoon extra virgin olive oil
8 spring onions (scallions), finely
  sliced
2 celery stalks, finely sliced
12 baby (dutch) carrots, sliced
310 g (2 bunches) asparagus,
  woody ends removed, cut into
  3 cm (1 1/4 inch) lengths
150 g (5 1/2 oz) baby corn, cut into
  3 cm (1 1/4 inch) lengths
60 g (1/4 cup) fresh or bottled pesto
extra virgin olive oil, to thin pesto
  (see Note)
shaved Parmesan cheese, to garnish

Bring the stock to the boil in a large
saucepan. Meanwhile, heat the olive
oil in a large heavy-based saucepan
and add the spring onion and celery.
Cover and cook over medium heat
for 5 minutes, or until softened.

Add the stock to the spring onion
mixture and mix well.

Add the carrot, asparagus and corn
to the pan. Return the mixture to the
boil, then reduce the heat and simmer
for 10 minutes.

Spoon into warmed soup bowls.
Top with a dollop of pesto, season
to taste with salt and pepper, and
garnish with shaved Parmesan.

Serves 4

Note: Home-made pesto or fresh
pesto from a deli will give a better
flavour than bottled pesto. If you
prefer a thinner pesto, mix it with
a little olive oil to give it a runnier
consistency.

Chilled garlic and almond soup

1 loaf (200 g/7 oz) day-old white
   Italian bread, crust removed
155 g (1 cup) whole blanched
   almonds
3–4 garlic cloves, chopped
125 ml (½ cup) extra virgin olive oil
80 ml (⅓ cup) sherry or white wine
   vinegar
315–375 ml (1¼–1½ cups) vegetable
   stock
2 tablespoons olive oil, extra
75 g (2½ oz) day-old white Italian
   bread, extra, crust removed, cut
   into 1 cm (½ inch) cubes
200 g (7 oz) small seedless green
   grapes

Soak the bread in cold water for
5 minutes, then squeeze out any
excess liquid. Chop the almonds and
garlic in a processor until well ground.
Add the bread and process until the
mixture is smooth.

With the motor running, add the olive
oil in a steady slow stream until the
mixture is the consistency of thick
mayonnaise. Slowly add the sherry
and 315 ml (1¼ cups) of the stock.
Blend for 1 minute. Season with salt.
Refrigerate for at least 2 hours. The
soup thickens on refrigeration so you
may need to add extra stock or water
to thin it.

When ready to serve, heat the extra
oil in a frying pan, add the bread
cubes and toss over medium heat
for 2–3 minutes, or until golden. Drain
on crumpled paper towels. Serve the
soup very cold, garnished with the
grapes and bread cubes.

Serves 4–6

Spinach soup

30 g (1 oz) butter
1 onion, finely chopped
500 g (1 lb 2 oz) floury potatoes,
  grated
1 litre (4 cups) vegetable or
  chicken stock
500 g (1 lb 2 oz) frozen chopped
  English spinach
1/4 teaspoon ground nutmeg
sour cream, to serve

Melt the butter in a large saucepan, add the chopped onion and cook, stirring occasionally, until soft but not browned.

Add the potato and stock to the pan and mix well, scraping the onion from the bottom of the pan. Add the unthawed blocks of spinach and cook, covered, until the spinach has thawed and broken up, stirring occasionally. Uncover and simmer for 10–15 minutes, or until the potato is very soft. Stir the soup frequently while it cooks to prevent sticking on the bottom. Transfer to a blender or food processor and blend in batches until smooth.

Return the soup to the pan and gently reheat. Add the nutmeg, and season with salt and black pepper. Ladle into bowls, add a dollop of sour cream to each bowl and swirl into the soup.

Serves 4

Zuppa di faggioli

2 x 400 g (14 oz) tins cannellini
  beans
1 tablespoon extra virgin olive oil
1 leek, finely chopped
2 garlic cloves, crushed
1 teaspoon thyme leaves
2 celery stalks, diced
1 carrot, diced
1 kg (2 lb 4 oz) silverbeet
  (Swiss chard), trimmed and
  roughly chopped
1 ripe tomato, diced
1 litre (4 cups) vegetable stock
2 small crusty rolls, each cut into
  4 slices
2 teaspoons balsamic vinegar
35 g (1/3 cup) finely grated Parmesan
  cheese

Put one tin of beans and liquid in a blender or small food processor and blend until smooth. Drain the other tin, reserving the beans and discarding the liquid.

Heat the oil in a large heavy-based saucepan, add the leek, garlic and thyme and cook for 2–3 minutes, or until soft and aromatic. Add the celery, carrot, silverbeet and tomato and cook for a further 2–3 minutes, or until the silverbeet has wilted. Heat the stock in a separate saucepan.

Stir the puréed cannellini beans and stock into the vegetable mixture. Bring to the boil, then reduce the heat and simmer for 5–10 minutes, or until the vegetables are tender. Add the drained beans and stir until heated through. Season to taste with salt and cracked black pepper.

Arrange 2 slices of bread in the base of each soup bowl. Stir the balsamic vinegar into the soup and ladle over the bread. Serve topped with grated Parmesan.

Serves 4

Note: This recipe is the authentic bean soup from Florence. If you like, spice it up by adding chopped chilli.

Split pea and vegetable soup

1 tablespoon peanut or
  vegetable oil
1 onion, chopped
2 garlic cloves, chopped
1 1/2 teaspoons chopped fresh
  ginger
1 1/2 tablespoons Madras curry
  paste
100 g (3 1/2 oz) yellow split peas,
  rinsed and drained
1 large zucchini (courgette), peeled
  and chopped
1 large carrot, roughly chopped
170 g (6 oz) button mushrooms,
  roughly chopped
1 celery stalk, roughly chopped
1 litre (4 cups) vegetable stock
125 ml (1/2 cup) cream

Heat the oil in a saucepan, add the onion and cook over low heat for 5 minutes, or until soft. Add the garlic, ginger and curry paste and cook over medium heat for 2 minutes. Stir in the split peas until well coated with paste, then add the zucchini, carrot, mushroom and celery and cook for 2 minutes.

Add the stock, bring to the boil, then reduce the heat and simmer, partly covered, for 1 hour. Remove from the heat and allow to cool slightly.

Transfer the soup to a blender or food processor and process in batches until smooth. Return to the pan, stir in the cream and gently heat until warmed through. Delicious served with naan bread.

Serves 4

Capsicum, spinach and chickpea soup

1 tablespoon olive oil
8 spring onions (scallions), finely sliced
1 red capsicum (pepper)
1 garlic clove, crushed
1 teaspoon cumin seeds
375 ml (1½ cups) Italian tomato passata
750 ml (3 cups) vegetable or beef stock
300 g (10½ oz) tin chickpeas, rinsed and drained
2 teaspoons red wine vinegar
1–2 teaspoons sugar
100 g (3½ oz) baby English spinach leaves

Heat the oil in a large heavy-based saucepan and stir in the spring onion. Reduce the heat and cook, covered, for 2–3 minutes, or until softened. Meanwhile, remove the seeds and membrane from the capsicum and finely dice. Add the capsicum, garlic and cumin seeds to the pan and cook for 1 minute.

Add the passata and stock and bring the mixture to the boil. Reduce the heat and simmer for 10 minutes. Add the chickpeas, vinegar and sugar to the soup and simmer for a further 5 minutes.

Stir in the baby spinach and season to taste with salt and ground black pepper. Cook until the spinach begins to wilt, then serve immediately.

Serves 4

Cream of fennel and leek soup

30 g (1 oz) butter
2 large fennel bulbs, thinly sliced
2 leeks, thinly sliced
1 litre (4 cups) hot vegetable or
  chicken stock
2 rosemary sprigs
1/8 teaspoon ground nutmeg
80 g (1/3 cup) sour cream
25 g (1/4 cup) finely grated Parmesan
  cheese
1 tablespoon oil
1 leek, extra, cut in half lengthways,
  and cut into 4 cm (1 1/2 inch) lengths
grated Parmesan cheese, extra,
  to garnish
sour cream, extra, to garnish

Heat the butter in a large heavy-based saucepan, add the sliced fennel and leek, and cook, covered, over medium heat for 2–3 minutes, stirring occasionally.

Put the hot stock, rosemary sprigs and nutmeg in a saucepan and bring to the boil. Simmer over low heat for about 15 minutes, then remove the rosemary sprigs and add the fennel and leek mixture to the pan.

Transfer the soup to a blender or food processor and blend in batches until smooth. Return to the pan, and stir in the sour cream and Parmesan. Reheat over medium heat until hot. Season to taste with salt and cracked black pepper and keep warm.

Heat the oil in a frying pan and cook the extra leek for 2–3 minutes, or until soft but not browned.

Spoon the soup into six warm soup bowls and top with the fried leek. Garnish with the extra Parmesan and sour cream and serve immediately.

Serves 6

Fresh mushroom, shallot and sour cream soup

2 tablespoons butter
100 g (about 4) French shallots,
   roughly chopped
3 garlic cloves, crushed
30 g (1 cup) firmly packed flat-leaf
   (Italian) parsley
315 ml (1 1/4 cups) vegetable or
   chicken stock
315 ml (1 1/4 cups) milk
600 g (1 lb 5 oz) button mushrooms
1/4 teaspoon ground nutmeg
1/4 teaspoon cayenne pepper
150 g (5 1/2 oz) light sour cream
cayenne pepper, to garnish

Melt the butter in a large heavy-based saucepan and add the shallots, garlic and parsley. Cook over medium heat for 2–3 minutes. Put the stock and milk in a separate saucepan and bring to the boil.

Gently wipe the mushrooms, then chop and add to the shallot mixture. Season with salt and pepper, and stir in the nutmeg and cayenne pepper. Cook, stirring, for 1 minute. Add the stock and milk, bring to the boil, then reduce the heat and simmer for 5 minutes. Transfer the soup to a blender or food processor and blend until smooth. Return to the pan.

Stir in the sour cream, adjust the seasoning and reheat gently. Serve sprinkled with cayenne pepper.

Serves 4

Note: For an ideal garnish, fry diced button mushrooms in a little butter until golden. This can be prepared during the soup's final simmering.

Asian noodle soup

8 dried Chinese mushrooms
100 g (3½ oz) dried rice vermicelli
800 g (1 lb 12 oz) Chinese broccoli,
  cut into 5 cm (2 inch) lengths
8 fried tofu puffs, cut into strips
125 g (4½ oz) bean sprouts
1 litre (4 cups) vegetable stock
2 tablespoons light soy sauce
1½ tablespoons Chinese rice wine
3 spring onions (scallions), finely
  chopped
coriander (cilantro) leaves, to serve

Place the dried mushrooms in a bowl, cover with boiling water and soak for 15 minutes. Drain, reserving 125 ml (½ cup) of the liquid. Squeeze the mushrooms to remove any excess liquid. Discard the stems and thinly slice the caps.

Soak the vermicelli in boiling water for 5 minutes. Drain. Divide the vermicelli, broccoli, tofu puffs and bean sprouts among the four serving bowls.

Place the reserved mushroom liquid, stock, soy sauce, rice wine, spring onion and mushrooms in a saucepan and bring to the boil. Cook, covered, for 10 minutes.

Ladle the soup into the serving bowls and garnish with the coriander leaves.

Serves 4

Vegetable and lentil soup with spiced yoghurt

2 tablespoons olive oil
1 small leek, white part only, chopped
2 garlic cloves, crushed
2 teaspoons curry powder
1 teaspoon ground cumin
1 teaspoon garam masala
1 litre (4 cups) vegetable stock
1 bay leaf
185 g (1 cup) brown lentils
450 g (1 lb) butternut pumpkin (squash), peeled and cut into 1 cm (½ inch) cubes
2 zucchini (courgettes), cut in half lengthways and sliced
400 g (14 oz) tin chopped tomatoes
200 g (7 oz) broccoli, cut into small florets
1 small carrot, diced
80 g (½ cup) peas
1 tablespoon chopped mint

Spiced yoghurt
250 g (1 cup) thick plain yoghurt
1 tablespoon chopped coriander (cilantro) leaves
1 garlic clove, crushed
3 dashes Tabasco sauce

Heat the oil in a saucepan over medium heat. Add the leek and garlic and cook for 4–5 minutes, or until soft and lightly golden. Add the curry powder, cumin and garam masala and cook for 1 minute, or until fragrant.

Add the stock, bay leaf, lentils and pumpkin. Bring to the boil, then reduce the heat to low and simmer for 10–15 minutes, or until the lentils are tender. Season well.

Add the zucchini, tomatoes, broccoli, carrot and 500 ml (2 cups) water and simmer for 10 minutes, or until the vegetables are tender. Add the peas and simmer for 2–3 minutes.

To make the spiced yoghurt, place the yoghurt, coriander, garlic and Tabasco in a small bowl and stir until combined.

Dollop a spoonful of the yoghurt on each serving of soup and garnish with the chopped mint.

Serves 6

Pumpkin soup

500 ml (2 cups) vegetable stock
750 g (1 ib 10 oz) butternut pumpkin
   (squash), cut into 1.5 cm (⁵/₈ inch)
   cubes
2 onions, chopped
2 garlic cloves, halved
¼ teaspoon ground nutmeg
60 ml (¼ cup) cream

Put the stock and 500 ml (2 cups) water in a large heavy-based saucepan and bring to the boil. Add the pumpkin, onion and garlic and return to the boil. Reduce the heat slightly and cook for 15 minutes, or until the pumpkin is soft.

Drain the vegetables through a colander, reserving the liquid. Purée the pumpkin mixture in a blender until smooth (you may need to add some of the reserved liquid). Return the pumpkin purée to the pan and stir in enough of the reserved liquid to reach the desired consistency. Season to taste with nutmeg, salt and cracked black pepper.

Ladle the soup into four soup bowls and pour some cream into each bowl to create a swirl pattern on the top. Serve with warm crusty bread.

Serves 4

Potato and rocket soup

1.5 litres (6 cups) vegetable or
  chicken stock
1.25 kg (2 lb 12 oz) desiree potatoes,
  chopped into small pieces
2 large garlic cloves, peeled, left
  whole
250 g (9 oz) rocket (arugula)
1 tablespoon extra virgin olive oil
extra rocket (arugula) leaves, to
  garnish (optional)
50 g (½ cup) shaved Parmesan
  cheese

Place the stock in a large heavy-
based saucepan and bring to the boil.
Add the potato and garlic and simmer
over medium heat for 15 minutes, or
until the potato is tender to the point
of a sharp knife. Add the rocket and
simmer for a further 2 minutes. Stir
in the olive oil.

Transfer the mixture to a blender or
food processor and blend in batches
until smooth. Return the mixture to
the pan and stir over medium heat
until hot. Season to taste with salt
and cracked black pepper and serve
in warmed bowls. Garnish with the
rocket leaves and shaved Parmesan
before serving.

Serves 6

Broth with ravioli

750 ml (3 cups) vegetable or
  chicken stock
250 g (9 oz) spinach and ricotta
  ravioli
85 g (3 oz) snowpeas (mangetout),
  sliced on the diagonal
2 tablespoons chopped flat-leaf
  (Italian) parsley
2 tablespoons chopped basil
grated Parmesan cheese,
  to garnish

Place the stock in a large heavy-based saucepan and bring to the boil. Add the ravioli and cook for 8–10 minutes, or until the pasta is *al dente*.

Season to taste with salt and pepper, and stir in the snowpeas, parsley and basil. Pour the soup into two bowls and sprinkle with grated Parmesan before serving.

Serves 2

Cold spicy roast capsicum soup

4 red capsicums (peppers)
2 teaspoons oil
2 garlic cloves, crushed
4 spring onions (scallions), sliced
1 teaspoon finely chopped seeded chillies
425 g (15 oz) tin crushed tomatoes
125 ml (½ cup) chilled vegetable stock
1 teaspoon balsamic vinegar
2 tablespoons chopped basil

Cut the capsicums into quarters and remove the seeds and membrane. Place the capsicums skin-side up under a hot grill (broiler) and grill until the skins blacken and blister. Cool in a plastic bag, then peel away the skin and roughly chop the flesh.

Heat the oil in a small saucepan, add the garlic, spring onion and chilli, and cook over low heat for 1–2 minutes, or until softened.

Transfer to a food processor or blender, and add the capsicum, crushed tomatoes and stock. Blend until smooth, then stir in the vinegar and basil. Season to taste with salt and cracked pepper. Refrigerate, then serve cold.

Serves 4

Sweet potato and chilli soup

1 tablespoon oil
1 onion, chopped
2 garlic cloves, finely chopped
1–2 small red chillies, finely chopped
1/4 teaspoon paprika
750 g (1 lb 10 oz) orange sweet
  potato, chopped into small pieces
1 litre (4 cups) vegetable or beef stock
chopped dried chilli, to garnish

Heat the oil in a large heavy-based saucepan, add the onion and cook for 1–2 minutes, or until soft. Add the garlic, chilli and paprika and cook for a further 2 minutes, or until aromatic. Add the sweet potato to the pan and toss to coat with the spices.

Pour in the stock, bring to the boil, then reduce the heat and simmer for 15 minutes, or until the vegetables are tender. Cool slightly, then transfer to a blender or food processor and blend in batches until smooth, adding extra water if needed to reach the desired consistency. Do not overblend or the mixture may become gluey.

Season to taste with salt and black pepper. Ladle the soup into bowls, sprinkle with dried chilli and serve.

Serves 4

Zucchini pesto soup

1 tablespoon olive oil
1 large onion, finely chopped
2 garlic cloves, crushed
750 ml (3 cups) vegetable or
  chicken stock
750 g (1 lb 10 oz) zucchini
  (courgettes), thinly sliced
60 ml (1/4 cup) cream
toasted ciabatta bread, to serve

Pesto
50 g (1 cup) basil
25 g (1/4 cup) finely grated
  Parmesan cheese
2 tablespoons pine nuts, toasted
2 tablespoons extra virgin olive oil

Heat the oil in a large heavy-based saucepan. Add the onion and garlic and cook over medium heat for 5 minutes, or until the onion is soft.

Bring the stock to the boil in a separate saucepan. Add the zucchini and hot stock to the onion mixture. Bring to the boil, then reduce the heat, cover and simmer for about 10 minutes, or until the zucchini is very soft.

To make the pesto, process the basil, Parmesan and pine nuts in a food processor for 20 seconds, or until finely chopped. Gradually add the olive oil and process until smooth. Spoon into a small bowl.

Transfer the zucchini mixture to a blender or food processor and blend in batches until smooth. Return the mixture to the pan, stir in the cream and 2 tablespoons of the pesto, and reheat over medium heat until hot. Season with salt and black pepper and serve with toasted ciabatta bread. Serve the remaining pesto in a bowl for diners to help themselves, or cover with olive oil and store in the refrigerator for up to 1 week.

Serves 4

Minestrone

80 g (1/2 cup) macaroni
1 tablespoon olive oil
1 leek, sliced
2 garlic cloves, crushed
1 carrot, sliced
1 waxy potato, chopped
1 zucchini (courgette), sliced
2 celery stalks, sliced
100 g (3 1/2 oz) green beans, cut
   into short lengths
425 g (15 oz) tin chopped tomatoes
2 litres (8 cups) vegetable or beef
   stock
2 tablespoons tomato paste (purée)
425 g (15 oz) tin cannellini beans,
   rinsed and drained
2 tablespoons chopped flat-leaf
   (Italian) parsley
shaved Parmesan cheese, to serve

Bring a saucepan of water to the boil, add the macaroni and cook for 10–12 minutes, or until tender. Drain.

Meanwhile, heat the oil in a large heavy-based saucepan, add the leek and garlic and cook over medium heat for 3–4 minutes.

Add the carrot, potato, zucchini, celery, green beans, tomato, stock and tomato paste. Bring to the boil, then reduce the heat and simmer for 10 minutes, or until the vegetables are tender.

Stir in the cooked pasta and cannellini beans and heat through. Spoon into warmed serving bowls and garnish with parsley and shaved Parmesan.

Serves 4

Note: Just about any vegetable can be added to minestrone, so this is a great recipe for using up odds and ends.

Chickpea, potato and spinach soup

1 litre (4 cups) vegetable stock
1½ tablespoons olive oil
1 onion, finely chopped
1 large potato, cut into 1.5 cm
 (⁵⁄₈ inch) cubes
1½ teaspoons paprika
2 garlic cloves, crushed
400 g (14 oz) tin chickpeas,
 drained
1 large tomato, cut into small
 cubes
50 g (1 cup) English spinach,
 coarsely shredded
25 g (¼ cup) grated Parmesan
 cheese

Place the stock in a saucepan, then cover and slowly bring to the boil. Heat the olive oil in a large heavy-based saucepan, and cook the onion for 2–3 minutes, or until soft.

Add the potato to the onion, and stir in the paprika, garlic and chickpeas. Add the onion mixture to the stock and bring to the boil. Stir in the tomato, and season with salt and cracked black pepper.

Simmer for 10 minutes, or until the potato is tender. Add the spinach and cook until wilted. Top with Parmesan, season to taste and serve.

Serves 4

Saffron and Jerusalem artichoke soup

1 pinch saffron threads
250 g (9 oz) Jerusalem artichokes
2 tablespoons lemon juice
1 tablespoon olive oil
1 large onion, finely chopped
1 litre (4 cups) vegetable or chicken
  stock
3 teaspoons ground cumin
500 g (1 lb 2 oz) desiree potatoes,
  grated
2 teaspoons lemon juice, extra

Place the saffron threads in a bowl with 2 tablespoons boiling water and leave until needed. Peel and thinly slice the artichokes, dropping the slices into a bowl of water mixed with lemon juice to prevent discolouration.

Heat the oil in a large heavy-based saucepan, add the onion and cook over medium heat for 2–3 minutes, or until the onion is softened. Bring the stock to the boil in a separate saucepan. Add the cumin to the onion mixture and cook for a further 30 seconds, or until fragrant. Add the drained artichokes, potato, saffron mixture, stock and extra lemon juice. Bring to the boil, then reduce the heat and simmer for 15–18 minutes, or until the artichokes are very soft.

Transfer to a blender and process in batches until smooth. Return the soup to the pan and season to taste with salt and cracked pepper. Reheat over medium heat and serve.

Serves 4

Salads

Moroccan carrot salad with green olives and mint

1½ teaspoons cumin seeds
½ teaspoon coriander seeds
1 tablespoon red wine vinegar
2 tablespoons olive oil
1 garlic clove, crushed
2 teaspoons harissa
¼ teaspoon orange flower water
600 g (1 lb 5 oz) baby (dutch) carrots, tops trimmed, well scrubbed
40 g (⅓ cup) large green olives, pitted and finely sliced
2 tablespoons shredded mint
30 g (1 cup) picked watercress leaves

In a small frying pan, dry-fry the cumin and coriander seeds for 30 seconds or until fragrant. Cool and then grind in a mortar and pestle or spice grinder. Place into a large mixing bowl with the red wine vinegar, olive oil, garlic, harissa and orange flower water. Whisk to combine.

Blanch the carrots in boiling salted water for 5 minutes, until almost tender. Drain into a colander and allow to sit for a few minutes until they dry. While still hot, add to the red wine vinegar dressing, and toss gently to coat. Allow to cool to room temperature, for the dressing to infuse into the carrots. Add the green olives and mint. Season well and toss gently to combine. Serve on the watercress leaves.

Serves 4

Roasted beet salad

2 tablespoons red wine vinegar
80 ml (1/3 cup) walnut oil
1 garlic clove, crushed
1 teaspoon Dijon mustard
12 French shallots
12 garlic cloves
6 medium beetroot, scrubbed well
1 tablespoon vegetable oil
70 g (2 cups) baby beetroot leaves
50 g (1/2 cup) walnuts, toasted

Preheat the oven to 200°C (400°F/ Gas 6). In a small bowl whisk together the red wine vinegar, walnut oil, garlic, and Dijon mustard. Season well with sea salt and pepper. Set aside.

Roast the shallots, garlic and beetroot for 1 hour. Remove from the oven and continue to roast the beetroot for a further 30 minutes, or until tender when pierced with a skewer.

Slip the shallots and garlic from their skin, and cut the beetroot into wedges. Add the dressing to the vegetables, toss together, and cool to room temperature.

In a large bowl, place the beet leaves, walnuts and vegetables with the dressing, season well with sea salt and pepper and gently toss together. Arrange on a serving platter, or individual plates.

Serves 4

Chargrilled cauliflower salad with sesame dressing

Sesame dressing
3 tablespoons tahini
1 garlic clove, crushed
60 ml (¼ cup) seasoned rice
  wine vinegar
1 tablespoon vegetable oil
1 teaspoon lime juice
¼ teaspoon sesame oil

1 medium head cauliflower
12 garlic cloves, crushed
2 tablespoons vegetable oil
2 baby cos (romaine) lettuces,
  washed well and drained
50 g (1¾ oz) picked watercress
  leaves, washed well and drained
2 teaspoons sesame seeds, toasted
1 tablespoon finely chopped parsley

Preheat the chargrill pan (griddle) or barbecue hotplate to medium heat. In a medium non-metallic bowl, place the tahini, garlic, rice wine vinegar, vegetable oil, lime juice, sesame oil and 1 tablespoon water. Whisk together thoroughly until well combined, and season to taste.

Cut the cauliflower in half, and then into 1 cm (½ inch) wedges. Place on a tray and gently rub with the garlic and vegetable oil. Season well. Chargrill the cauliflower pieces until golden on both sides and cooked through. Remove from the chargrill pan.

Arrange the cos leaves and watercress on a serving platter and top with the chargrilled cauliflower slices. Drizzle the dressing over the top and garnish with the sesame seeds and parsley. Serve immediately.

Serves 4

Thai green papaya salad

500 g (1 lb 2 oz) green papaya,
  peeled and seeded
1–2 small red chillies, thinly sliced
1 tablespoon grated palm sugar
1 tablespoon soy sauce
2 tablespoons lime juice
1 tablespoon fried garlic (see Note)
1 tablespoon fried shallots (see Note)
50 g (1 3/4 oz) green beans, cut into
  1 cm (1/2 inch) lengths
8 cherry tomatoes, quartered
2 tablespoons chopped roasted
  unsalted peanuts

Grate the papaya into long, fine shreds with a zester or a knife.

Place the papaya in a large mortar and pestle with the chilli, palm sugar, soy sauce and lime juice. Lightly pound until combined. Add the fried garlic and shallots, beans and tomatoes. Lightly pound for a further minute, or until combined. Serve immediately, sprinkled with the peanuts.

Serves 4

Note: Packets of fried garlic and shallots are available from Asian food stores.

Warm casarecci and sweet potato salad

750 g (1 lb 10 oz) orange sweet potato
2 tablespoons extra virgin olive oil
500 g (1 lb 2 oz) casarecci pasta
325 g (11½ oz) marinated feta cheese in oil
3 tablespoons balsamic vinegar
155 g (1 bunch) asparagus, cut into short lengths
100 g (3½ oz) baby rocket (arugula) or baby English spinach leaves
2 vine-ripened tomatoes, chopped
40 g (¼ cup) pine nuts, toasted

Preheat the oven to 200°C (400°F/ Gas 6). Peel the sweet potato and cut into large pieces. Place in a baking dish, drizzle with the olive oil and season generously with salt and cracked black pepper. Bake for 20 minutes, or until the sweet potato is tender.

Cook the pasta in a large saucepan of rapidly boiling water until *al dente*. Drain well.

Drain the oil from the feta and whisk 3 tablespoons of the oil together with the balsamic vinegar to make a dressing.

Steam the asparagus until bright green and tender. Drain well.

Combine the pasta, sweet potato, asparagus, rocket, feta, tomatoes and pine nuts in a bowl. Add the dressing and toss gently. Season with black pepper and serve immediately.

Serves 4

Insalata caprese

3 large vine-ripened tomatoes
250 g (9 oz) bocconcini
12 basil leaves
60 ml (¼ cup) extra virgin olive oil
4 basil leaves, roughly torn, extra

Slice the tomato into twelve 1 cm (½ inch) slices. Slice the bocconcini into 24 slices the same thickness as the tomato.

Arrange the tomato slices on a plate, alternating them with 2 slices of bocconcini and placing a basil leaf between the bocconcini slices.

Drizzle with the olive oil, sprinkle with the torn basil and season well with salt and freshly ground black pepper

Serves 4

Note: You could use whole cherry tomatoes and toss them with the bocconcini and basil.

Warm potato salad with green olive dressing

1.5 kg (3 lb 5 oz) nicola potatoes, scrubbed (or any small, waxy potato)
90 g (½ cup) green olives, pitted and finely chopped
2 teaspoons capers, finely chopped
15 g (¾ cup) parsley, finely chopped
2 tablespoons lemon juice
1 teaspoon finely grated lemon zest
2 garlic cloves, crushed
125 ml (½ cup) extra virgin olive oil

Boil the potatoes for 15 minutes or until just tender (pierce with the tip of a sharp knife — if the potato comes away easily it is ready). Drain and cool slightly.

While the potatoes are cooking, place the olives and capers in a small bowl with the parsley, lemon juice, lemon zest, garlic and olive oil. Whisk with a fork to combine.

Cut the potatoes into halves and gently toss with the dressing while still warm. Taste before seasoning with fresh black pepper and a little salt, if required.

Serves 6

Gado gado

2 small carrots, thinly sliced
100 g (3½ oz) cauliflower, cut into
  small florets
60 g (2¼ oz) snowpeas (mangetout),
  trimmed
100 g (3½ oz) bean sprouts
8 well-shaped iceberg lettuce leaves
4 small potatoes, cooked and cut into
  thin slices
1 Lebanese (short) cucumber, thinly
  sliced
2 hard-boiled eggs, peeled and cut
  into quarters
2 ripe tomatoes, cut into wedges

Peanut sauce
1 tablespoon oil
1 small onion, finely chopped
125 g (½ cup) crunchy peanut butter
185 ml (¾ cup) coconut milk
1 teaspoon sambal oelek
1 tablespoon lemon juice
1 tablespoon kecap manis

Steam the carrots and cauliflower in a saucepan for 5 minutes, or until nearly tender. Add the snowpeas and cook for 2 minutes. Add the bean sprouts and cook for a further 1 minute. Remove from the heat and cool.

To make the peanut sauce, heat the oil in a saucepan and cook the onion for 5 minutes over low heat, or until soft and lightly golden. Add the peanut butter, coconut milk, sambal oelek, lemon juice, kecap manis and 60 ml (¼ cup) water, and stir well. Bring to the boil, stirring constantly, then reduce the heat and simmer for 5 minutes, or until the sauce has reduced and thickened. Remove from the heat.

Place two lettuce leaves together (one inside the other) to make 4 lettuce cups.

In each lettuce cup, arrange one quarter of the potato, carrot, cauliflower, snowpeas, bean sprouts and cucumber. Top with some of the peanut sauce, and garnish with the egg and tomato.

Serves 4

Roasted fennel and orange salad

8 baby fennel bulbs
5 tablespoons olive oil
2 oranges
1 tablespoon lemon juice
1 red onion, halved and thinly sliced
100 g (3½ oz) Kalamata olives
2 tablespoons roughly chopped mint
1 tablespoon roughly chopped
   flat-leaf (Italian) parsley

Preheat the oven to 200°C (400°F/ Gas 6). Trim the fronds from the fennel and reserve. Remove the stalks and cut a slice off the base of each fennel 5 mm (¼ inch) thick. Slice each fennel into 6 wedges, put iin a baking dish and drizzle with 3 tablespoons olive oil. Season well. Bake for 40–45 minutes, or until tender and slightly caramelized. Turn once or twice during cooking. Allow to cool.

Cut a thin slice off the top and bottom of each orange. Using a sharp knife, slice off the skin and pith. Remove as much pith as possible. Slice down the side of a segment between the flesh and the membrane. Repeat with the other side and lift the segment out. Do this over a bowl to catch the juices. Repeat with all the segments on both oranges. Squeeze out any juice remaining in the membranes.

Whisk the remaining oil into the orange juice and the lemon juice until emulsified. Season well. Combine the orange segments, onion and olives in a bowl, pour on half the dressing and add half the mint. Mix well. Transfer to a serving dish. Top with the fennel, drizzle with the remaining dressing, and scatter the parsley and remaining mint over the top. Chop the reserved fronds and sprinkle over the salad.

Serves 4

Tabbouleh

130 g (³/₄ cup) burghul
3 ripe tomatoes
1 telegraph cucumber
4 spring onions (scallions), sliced
120 g (4 cups) chopped flat-leaf
  (Italian) parsley
25 g (½ cup) chopped mint

Dressing
80 ml (⅓ cup) lemon juice
60 ml (¼ cup) olive oil
1 tablespoon extra virgin olive oil

Place the burghul in a bowl, cover with 500 ml (2 cups) water and leave for 1½ hours.

Cut the tomatoes in half, squeeze to remove any excess seeds and cut into 1 cm (½ inch) cubes. Cut the cucumber in half lengthways, remove the seeds with a teaspoon and cut the flesh into 1 cm (½ inch) cubes.

To make the dressing, place the lemon juice and 1½ teaspoons salt in a bowl and whisk until well combined. Season well with freshly ground black pepper and slowly whisk in the olive oil and extra virgin olive oil.

Drain the burghul and squeeze out any excess water. Spread the burghul out on a clean tea towel or paper towels and leave to dry for about 30 minutes. Put the burghul in a large salad bowl, add the tomato, cucumber, spring onion, parsley and mint, and toss well to combine.

Pour the dressing over the salad and toss until evenly coated.

Serves 6

Cucumber, feta, mint and dill salad

120 g (4 oz) feta cheese
4 Lebanese (short) cucumbers
1 small red onion, thinly sliced
1 1/2 tablespoons finely chopped dill
1 tablespoon dried mint
3 tablespoons olive oil
1 1/2 tablespoons lemon juice

Crumble the feta into 1 cm (1/2 inch) pieces and place in a large bowl. Peel and seed the cucumbers and cut into 1 cm (1/2 inch) dice. Add to the bowl along with the onion and dill.

Grind the mint in a mortar and pestle, or force through a sieve, until powdered. Combine with the oil and juice, then season with salt and black pepper. Pour over the salad and toss well.

Serves 4

Warm choy sum salad

370 g (13 oz) choy sum
2 tablespoons peanut oil
3 teaspoons finely grated ginger
2 garlic cloves, finely chopped
2 teaspoons sugar
2 teaspoons sesame oil
2 tablespoons soy sauce
1 tablespoon lemon juice
2 teaspoons seasame seeds, toasted

Trim the ends from the choy sum and slice in half. Steam for 2 minutes or until wilted and arrange on a serving plate.

Heat a small saucepan until very hot, add the peanut oil and swirl it around to coat the pan. Add the ginger and garlic and stir-fry for 1 minute. Add the sugar, sesame oil, soy sauce and lemon juice, heat until hot and pour over the choy sum. Season to taste, garnish with sesame seeds and serve immediately.

Serves 4

Cherry and pear tomato salad with white beans

3 tablespoons olive oil
2 red Asian shallots, finely diced
1 large garlic clove, crushed
1½ tablespoons lemon juice
250 g (9 oz) red cherry tomatoes, halved
250 g (9 oz) yellow pear tomatoes, halved
425 g (15 oz) tin white beans, drained and rinsed
20 g (⅓ cup) basil leaves, torn
2 tablespoons chopped parsley

Place the olive oil, diced shallots, crushed garlic and lemon juice into a small bowl and whisk to combine.

Place the halved cherry and pear tomatoes and the white beans in a serving bowl. Drizzle with the dr and scatter the basil and parsley over the top. Toss gently to combine.

Serves 4

Beetroot and chive salad

24 (1.5 kg/3 lb 5 oz) baby beetroot,
   unpeeled, trimmed and washed
50 g (½ cup) walnut halves
50 g (2 cups) roughly chopped
   watercress
1½ tablespoons snipped chives
   (2 cm/¾ inch lengths)

Dressing
¼ teaspoon honey
¼ teaspoon Dijon mustard
1 tablespoon balsamic vinegar
2 tablespoons olive oil

Preheat the oven to 200°C (400°F/ Gas 6). Place the beetroot in a roasting tin, cover with foil and roast for 1 hour, or until tender when pierced with a skewer. Remove from the oven and peel when cool enough to handle.

Meanwhile, for the dressing, combine the honey, mustard and balsamic vinegar in a small jug. Whisk in the oil with a fork until well combined and season to taste with salt and freshly ground black pepper.

Reduce the oven temperature to 180°C (350°F/Gas 4). Spread the walnuts on a baking tray and bake for 10 minutes, or until lightly golden. Keep a close watch on the nuts as they will burn easily. When cool, roughly chop the walnuts. Combine the watercress, beetroot and chives in a large bowl with the dressing and chopped walnuts and serve.

Serves 4

Snowpea salad with Japanese dressing

250 g (9 oz) snowpeas (mangetout), trimmed
iced water
50 g (1¾ oz) snowpea (mangetout) sprouts
1 small red capsicum (pepper), julienned
½ teaspoon dashi granules
1 tablespoon soy sauce
1 tablespoon mirin
1 teaspoon soft brown sugar
1 garlic clove, crushed
1 teaspoon very finely chopped ginger
¼ teaspoon sesame oil
1 tablespoon vegetable oil
1 tablespoon toasted sesame seeds

Bring a saucepan of water to the boil, add the snowpeas and cook for 1 minute. Drain, then plunge into a bowl of iced water for 2 minutes. Drain well and combine with the sprouts and capsicum in a serving bowl.

Dissolve the dashi granules in 1½ tablespoons of hot water and whisk in a small bowl with the soy sauce, mirin, sugar, garlic, ginger, sesame oil, vegetable oil and half of the toasted sesame seeds. Pour over the snowpea mixture and toss well. Season to taste, and serve sprinkled with the remaining sesame seeds.

Serves 4–6

Warm artichoke salad

8 young globe artichokes
(200 g/7 oz each)
1 lemon
25 g (1/2 cup) shredded basil
50 g (1/2 cup) shaved Parmesan
cheese

Dressing
1 garlic clove, finely chopped
1/2 teaspoon sugar
1 teaspoon Dijon mustard
2 teaspoons finely chopped lemon
zest
60 ml (1/4 cup) lemon juice
80 ml (1/3 cup) extra virgin olive oil

Remove the tough outer leaves from the artichokes until you get to the pale green leaves. Cut across the top of the artichoke, halfway down the tough leaves, then trim the stems to 4 cm (11/2 inches) long, and lightly peel them. Cut each artichoke in half lengthways and remove the hairy choke with a teaspoon. Rub each artichoke with lemon while you work and place in a bowl of cold water mixed with lemon juice to prevent the artichokes from turning brown.

Place the artichokes in a large saucepan of boiling water, top with a plate or heatproof bowl to keep them immersed, and cook for 25 minutes, or until tender. To check tenderness, place a skewer into the largest part of the artichoke. It should insert easily. Drain and cut in half again to serve.

For the dressing, mix the garlic, sugar, mustard, lemon zest and lemon juice in a jug. Season with salt and freshly ground black pepper, then whisk in the oil with a fork until combined. Pour over the artichoke and scatter with the basil and Parmesan.

Serves 4

Semi-dried tomato and baby spinach salad

2 quarters of preserved lemon
150 g (5½ oz) baby English spinach
  leaves
200 g (7 oz) semi-dried (sun-blushed)
  tomatoes, sliced
225 g (8 oz) jar marinated artichoke
  hearts, drained and sliced
85 g (½ cup) small black olives
2 tablespoons lemon juice
3 tablespoons olive oil
1 large garlic clove, crushed

Remove and discard the pith and flesh from the preserved lemon. Wash the zest and thinly slice. Place the spinach leaves in a bowl with the semi-dried tomatoes, artichoke hearts, black olives and the preserved lemon slices.

Place the lemon juice, olive oil and garlic in a bowl, season and mix well. Pour over the spinach mixture and toss to coat. Serve immediately.

Serves 6

Frisee and garlic crouton salad

Vinaigrette
1 French shallot, finely chopped
1 tablespoon Dijon mustard
60 ml (¼ cup) tarragon vinegar
170 ml (⅔ cup) extra virgin olive oil

1 tablespoon olive oil
½ medium bread stick, sliced
4 whole garlic cloves
1 baby frisee (curly endive), washed
  and dried
100 g (3½ oz) walnuts, toasted
100 g (3½ oz) feta cheese, crumbled

For the vinaigrette, whisk together in a bowl the shallot, mustard and vinegar. Slowly add the oil, whisking constantly until thickened. Set aside.

Heat the oil in a large frying pan, add the bread and garlic cloves and cook over medium–high heat for 5–8 minutes, until the croutons are crisp. Remove the garlic from the pan. Once the croutons are cool, break into small pieces.

Place the frisee, croutons, walnuts, feta cheese and vinaigrette in a large bowl. Toss together well and serve.

Serves 4–6

Steamed corn salad with Asian dressing

1 large red capsicum (pepper)
3 corn cobs, husks removed
90 g (1 cup) bean shoots
4 spring onions (scallions), thinly
  sliced on the diagonal

Asian dressing
1/2 teaspoon crushed garlic
1/2 teaspoon finely grated fresh ginger
1 teaspoon sugar
1 tablespoon rice vinegar
1 tablespoon soy sauce
1 tablespoon lemon juice
2 teaspoons sesame oil
2 tablespoons peanut oil

Cut the capsicum into large flattish pieces. Cook, skin-side up, under a hot grill (broiler) until the skin blackens and blisters. Place in a plastic bag and leave to cool, then peel away the skin and tear the capsicum into large strips.

Using a heavy knife, slice the cor into six 2.5 cm (1 inch) pieces. Steam for 5–8 minutes, or until tender. Arrange with the capsicum and bean shoots on a serving plate.

For the Asian dressing, mix the garlic, ginger, sugar, rice vinegar lemon juice together in a jug. Whisk in the oils with a fork until combined and season with pepper the salad and top with spring onion.

Serves 4

Eggplant and lentil salad

60 ml (¼ cup) olive oil
300 g (10½ oz) eggplant (aubergine),
    diced into 5 mm (¼ inch) cubes
1 small red onion, finely diced
¼ teaspoon ground cumin
3 garlic cloves, chopped
200 g (7 oz) puy lentils
375 ml (1½ cups) vegetable stock
2 tablespoons chopped parsley
1 tablespoon red wine vinegar
1 tablespoon extra virgin olive oil

Heat 2 tablespoons of olive oil in a large frying pan over medium heat. Add the eggplant and cook, stirring constantly, for 5 minutes, or until soft. Add the onion and cumin and cook for another 2–3 minutes, or until the onion has softened. Place the mixture in a bowl and season well.

Heat the remaining olive oil in the frying pan over medium heat. Add the garlic and cook for 1 minute. Add the lentils and stock and cook, stirring regularly, over low heat for 40 minutes, or until the liquid has evaporated and the lentils are tender.

Add the lentils to the bowl with the eggplant and stir in the parsley and red wine vinegar. Season well with salt and black pepper, drizzle with the extra virgin olive oil and serve warm.

Serves 4–6

Coleslaw with lime mayonnaise

2 egg yolks
1 tablespoon soy sauce
1 bird's eye chilli, finely chopped
3 tablespoons lime juice
200 ml (7 fl oz) olive oil
225 g (3 cups) shredded purple
    cabbage
225 g (3 cups) shredded white
    cabbage
160 g (1 cup) grated carrot
180 g (2 cups) bean sprouts
30 g (1 cup) coriander (cilantro)
    leaves, finely chopped
4 spring onions (scallions), finely
    sliced

To make the mayonnaise, place the egg yolks, soy sauce, chilli, a pinch of salt and the lime juice in the bowl of a food processor. With the motor running, very slowly add the olive oil to the egg yolk mixture, starting with a few drops at a time. When about half the oil has been added, pour the remaining oil in a steady stream until all has been incorporated. Add 1 tablespoon of warm water and stir well. Place the mayonnaise in a bowl, cover, and refrigerate until needed.

In a large bowl combine the cabbages, carrot, bean sprouts, coriander and spring onion. Toss well to combine all ingredients. Add the lime mayonnaise, stir to combine and serve.

Serves 4–6

Asparagus orange salad

300 g (10½ oz) thin asparagus spears
50 g (1½ cups) watercress
½ small red onion, very thinly sliced
1 orange, cut into 12 segments
1 tablespoon fresh orange juice
1 teaspoon finely grated orange zest
1 teaspoon sugar
1 tablespoon red wine vinegar
2 teaspoons poppy seeds
2 tablespoons olive oil
60 g (2¼ oz) soft goat's cheese

Cook the asparagus in boiling water for 1–2 minutes, or until just tender Rinse under cold water to cool, then combine with the watercress, r onion and orange segments on a serving dish.

Combine the orange juice, orange zest, sugar, red wine vinegar and poppy seeds in a jug. Whisk in the oil with a fork until combined and drizzle over the salad. Crumble the goat' cheese over the salad and season to taste with salt and pepper.

Serves 4

Red potato salad with dill and mustard dressing

6 medium (1.1 kg/2 lb 8 oz) waxy,
red-skinned potatoes (eg desiree)

Dill and mustard dressing
1 tablespoon seeded mustard
1½ tablespoons chopped dill
2 teaspoons soft brown sugar
60 ml (¼ cup) red wine vinegar
80 ml (⅓ cup) olive oil

Steam or boil the potatoes for
20 minutes, or until tender. Remove,
and when cool enough to handle,
cut into 3 cm (1¼ inch) chunks.

For the dill and mustard dressing,
mix the mustard, dill, brown sugar
and vinegar together in a jug. Whisk
in the oil with a fork until combined.
Toss through the warm potatoes,
and season with salt and pepper.

Serves 4

Salata baladi (Arabic fresh vegetable salad)

2 tablespoons extra virgin olive oil
2 tablespoons lemon juice
1 cos (romaine) lettuce, torn into
  bite-sized pieces
3 ripe tomatoes, each cut into
  8 pieces
1 green pepper (capsicum), cut into
  bite-sized pieces
1 telegraph cucumber, seeded and
  chopped
6 radishes, sliced
1 small salad or red onion, thinly
  sliced (see Note)
2 tablespoons chopped flat-leaf
  (Italian) parsley
2 tablespoons chopped mint

In a bowl, whisk together the olive oil
and lemon juice. Season well with salt
and pepper.

Combine the vegetables and herbs
in a serving bowl and toss well. Add
the dressing and toss to combine.

Serves 4–6

Note: Salad onions are sweeter
than normal onions and are
readily available.

Vietnamese salad with lemon grass dressing

200 g (7 oz) dried rice vermicelli
10 g (½ cup) torn Vietnamese mint
15 g (½ cup) coriander (cilantro)
  leaves
½ red onion, cut into thin wedges
1 green mango, cut into julienne strips
1 Lebanese (short) cucumber, halved
  lengthways and thinly sliced on
  the diagonal
140 g (1 cup) crushed peanuts

Lemon grass dressing
125 ml (½ cup) lime juice
1 tablespoon shaved palm sugar
60 ml (¼ cup) seasoned rice vinegar
2 stems lemon grass, finely chopped
2 red chillies, seeded and finely
  chopped
3 makrut (kaffir) lime leaves, shredded

Place the rice vermicelli in a bowl and cover with boiling water. Leave for 10 minutes, or until soft, then drain, rinse under cold water and cut into short lengths.

Place the vermicelli, mint, coriander, onion, mango, cucumber and three-quarters of the nuts in a large bowl and toss together.

To make the dressing, place all the ingredients in a jar with a lid and shake together.

Toss the dressing through the salad and refrigerate for 30 minutes. Sprinkle with the remaining nuts just before serving.

Serves 4–6

Mains

Artichoke risoni

30 g (1 oz) butter
1 tablespoon olive oil
2 fennel bulbs, sliced
340 g (12 oz) marinated artichoke
  hearts, drained and chopped
300 ml (10½ fl oz) cream
1 tablespoon Dijon mustard
3 tablespoons dry white wine
50 g (½ cup) grated Parmesan
  cheese
375 g (13 oz) risoni
130 g (2 cups) shredded English
  spinach

Heat the butter and oil in a frying pan over medium heat, add the fennel and cook for 20 minutes, or until caramelized. Add the artichoke and cook for 5–10 minutes longer. Stir in the cream, mustard, white wine and grated Parmesan and bring to the boil. Reduce the heat and simmer for 5 minutes.

Meanwhile, cook the pasta in a large saucepan of rapidly boiling water until *al dente*, then drain well.

Add the risoni and spinach to the sauce and cook until the spinach has wilted. This is delicious served with toasted Italian bread.

Serves 4

Baked sweet potato and watercress gnocchi

700 g (1 lb 9 oz) orange sweet potato
300 g (10½ oz) desiree potatoes
350 g (12 oz) plain (all-purpose) flour
35 g (⅓ cup) grated Parmesan cheese
30 g (1 cup) watercress leaves, finely chopped
1 garlic clove, crushed
60 g (2¼ oz) butter
25 g (¼ cup) grated Parmesan cheese, extra
2 tablespoons chopped parsley

Boil the sweet potato and desiree potatoes in their skin until tender. Drain, and when cool enough to handle, peel and press through a potato ricer or mouli into a bowl. Add the flour, grated Parmesan, watercress and garlic, and season well. Gently bring together with your hands until a soft dough forms. It is important not to overwork the dough to keep the gnocchi tender. Portion into walnut-size pieces and shape using the back of a fork to create the traditional 'gnocchi' shape.

Melt the butter in a large roasting tray. Preheat the grill (broiler) to medium–high heat.

Cook the gnocchi in a large saucepan of boiling salted water for 2 minutes, or until they rise to the surface. Scoop out with a slotted spoon, draining the water off well. Arrange in the roasting tray, tossing gently in the butter, and grill for 5 minutes, or until lightly golden. Sprinkle with the extra Parmesan and chopped parsley and serve immediately.

Serves 6

Couscous vegetable loaf

1 litre (4 cups) vegetable stock
500 g (1 lb 2 oz) instant couscous
30 g (1 oz) butter
3 tablespoons olive oil
2 garlic cloves, crushed
1 onion, finely chopped
1 tablespoon ground coriander
1 teaspoon ground cinnamon
1 teaspoon garam masala
250 g (9 oz) cherry tomatoes,
    quartered
1 zucchini (courgette), diced
130 g (4½ oz) tin corn kernels,
    drained
8 large basil leaves
150 g (5½ oz) sun-dried capsicums
    (peppers) in oil
60 g (1 cup) chopped basil, extra
80 ml (⅓ cup) orange juice
1 tablespoon lemon juice
3 tablespoons chopped flat-leaf
    (Italian) parsley
1 teaspoon honey
1 teaspoon ground cumin

Bring the vegetable stock to the boil in a saucepan. Place the couscous and butter in a bowl, cover with the stock and leave for 10 minutes.

Meanwhile, heat 1 tablespoon of the oil in a large frying pan and cook the garlic and onion over low heat for 5 minutes, or until the onion is soft. Add the spices and cook for 1 minute, or until fragrant. Remove from the pan. Add the remaining oil to the pan and cook the tomatoes, zucchini and corn over high heat until soft.

Line a 3 litre (12 cup) loaf tin with plastic wrap, letting it overhang the sides. Form the basil into two flowers on the base. Drain the capsicums, reserving 2 tablespoons of oil, then roughly chop. Add the onion mixture, tomato mixture, capsicum and extra basil to the couscous and mix. Cool.

Press the mixture into the tin and fold the plastic wrap over to cover. Weigh down with food tins and chill overnight.

To make the dressing, place the remaining ingredients and reserved capsicum oil in a jar with a lid and shake. Turn out the loaf, cut into slices and serve with the dressing.

Serves 6

Mushroom risotto

1.5 litres (6 cups) vegetable stock
500 ml (2 cups) white wine
2 tablespoons olive oil
60 g (2¼ oz) butter
1 leek, thinly sliced
500 g (1 lb 2 oz) flat mushrooms, sliced
500 g (2¼ cups) arborio rice
75 g (¾ cup) grated Parmesan cheese
3 tablespoons chopped flat-leaf (Italian) parsley
balsamic vinegar, to serve
shaved Parmesan cheese, to garnish
flat-leaf (Italian) parsley, to garnish

Place the stock and wine in a large saucepan, bring to the boil, then reduce the heat to low, cover and keep at a low simmer.

Heat the oil and butter in a large saucepan. Add the leek and cook over medium heat for 5 minutes, or until soft and golden. Add the mushrooms and cook for 5 minutes, or until tender. Stir in the arborio rice until it is translucent.

Add 125 ml (½ cup) stock, stirring constantly over medium heat until the liquid is absorbed. Continue adding more stock, 125 ml (½ cup) at a time, stirring constantly for 20–25 minutes, or until all the stock is absorbed and the rice is tender and creamy.

Stir in the Parmesan and chopped parsley until all the cheese is melted. Serve drizzled with vinegar and top with Parmesan shavings and parsley.

Serves 4

Eggplant, ricotta and pasta pots

200 g (7 oz) straight macaroni
125 ml (1/2 cup) light olive oil
1 large eggplant (aubergine), cut
  lengthways into 1 cm (1/2 inch)
  slices
1 small onion, finely chopped
2 garlic cloves, crushed
400 g (14 oz) tin diced tomatoes
400 g (14 oz) ricotta cheese
80 g (1 cup) coarsely grated
  Parmesan cheese
15 g (1/2 cup) shredded basil,
  plus extra to garnish

Preheat the oven to 180°C (350°F/ Gas 4). Cook the macaroni in a large saucepan of salted boiling water until *al dente*. Drain.

Heat 2 tablespoons of oil in a non-stick frying pan over medium heat. Cook the eggplant in three batches for 2–3 minutes each side, or until golden, adding 2 tablespoons of oil with each batch. Remove and drain well on crumpled paper towels. Add the onion and garlic to the frying pan and cook over medium heat for 2–3 minutes, or until just golden. Add the tomato and cook for 5 minutes, or until the sauce is pulpy and most of the liquid has evaporated. Season, then remove from the heat.

Combine the ricotta, Parmesan and basil in a large bowl, then mix in the pasta. Line the base and sides of four 375 ml (1 1/2 cup) ramekins with eggplant, trimming any overhanging pieces. Top with half the pasta mix, pressing down firmly. Spoon on the tomato sauce, then cover with the remaining pasta mixture. Bake for 10–15 minutes, or until heated through and golden on top. Stand for 5 minutes, then run a knife around the ramekin to loosen. Invert onto plates and garnish with a sprig of basil.

Serves 4

Frittata of zucchini flowers, oregano and ricotta salata

2 tablespoons olive oil
1 onion, finely chopped
2 garlic cloves, finely sliced
8 small zucchini (courgettes)
  with flowers
8 eggs, lightly whisked
7 g (1/4 cup) oregano, chopped
35 g (1/3 cup) ricotta salata, grated
  (see Note)
25 g (1/4 cup) grated Parmesan
  cheese
1 tablespoon shaved Parmesan
  cheese
lemon wedges, to serve

Preheat the oven to 200°C (400°F/ Gas 6). Heat the oil in an ovenproof 20 cm (8 inch) frying pan and cook the onion and garlic until softened. Arrange the zucchini flowers evenly in the pan, and add the egg. Sprinkle the oregano, ricotta salata and grated Parmesan over the top and season well with black pepper.

Put the pan in the oven and cook for about 10 minutes, or until set. Remove from the oven and allow to cool slightly. Top with the shaved Parmesan, cut into wedges and serve with a piece of lemon.

Serves 4

Note: Originating in Sicily, ricotta salata is a firm white rindless cheese with a nutty, sweet milky flavour. If unavailable, substitute with a mild feta cheese.

Phad Thai

400 g (14 oz) flat rice-stick noodles
2 tablespoons peanut oil
2 eggs, lightly beaten
1 onion, cut into thin wedges
2 garlic cloves, crushed
1 small red capsicum (pepper),
  cut into thin strips
100 g (3½ oz) fried tofu, cut into
  5 mm (¼ inch) wide strips
6 spring onions (scallions), thinly
  sliced on the diagonal
25 g (½ cup) chopped coriander
  (cilantro) leaves
60 ml (¼ cup) soy sauce
2 tablespoons lime juice
1 tablespoon soft brown sugar
2 teaspoons sambal oelek
90 g (1 cup) bean shoots
40 g (¼ cup) chopped roasted
  unsalted peanuts

Cook the noodles in a saucepan of boiling water for 5–10 minutes, or until tender. Drain and set aside.

Heat a wok over high heat and add enough peanut oil to coat the bottom and side. When smoking, add the egg and swirl to form a thin omelette. Cook for 30 seconds, or until just set. Roll up, remove and thinly slice.

Heat the remaining oil in the wok. Cook the onion, garlic and capsicum over high heat for 2–3 minutes, or until the onion has softened. Add the noodles, tossing well. Stir in the omelette, tofu, spring onion and half the coriander.

Pour in the combined soy sauce, lime juice, sugar and sambal oelek, then toss to coat the noodles. Sprinkle the bean shoots over the top and garnish with the peanuts and the remaining coriander. Serve immediately.

Serves 4

Casarecci pasta with roasted tomatoes, rocket and goat's cheese

16 Roma (plum) tomatoes
7 g (¼ cup) basil leaves, torn
400 g (14 oz) casarecci pasta
80 ml (⅓ cup) olive oil
2 garlic cloves, finely sliced
2 tablespoons lemon juice
120 g (4 cups) rocket (arugula),
  roughly chopped
2 tablespoons chopped parsley
35 g (⅓ cup) grated Parmesan
  cheese
100 g (3½ oz) goat's cheese

Preheat the oven to 160°C (315°F/ Gas 2–3). Score a cross in the base of the tomatoes. Place in a heatproof bowl, and cover with boiling water. Leave for 30 seconds, then transfer to cold water and peel the skin away from the cross. Cut in half and place cut-side up on a wire rack over a baking tray. Season liberally with salt and black pepper and scatter with the basil leaves. Put the tray in the oven and bake for 3 hours.

In a large saucepan of boiling salted water, cook the pasta until *al dente*. Drain and keep warm.

Heat the olive oil and garlic over low–medium heat until it just begins to sizzle. Remove immediately, and add to the pasta with the tomatoes, lemon juice, rocket, parsley and Parmesan. Stir gently to combine, allowing the heat from the pasta to wilt the rocket. Serve topped with crumbled goat's cheese.

Serves 4

Beetroot ravioli with sage burnt butter sauce

340 g (12 oz) jar baby beetroots
  in sweet vinegar
40 g (1½ oz) grated Parmesan
  cheese
250 g (9 oz) fresh ricotta cheese
750 g (1 lb 10 oz) fresh lasagne
  sheets (4 sheets)
fine cornmeal, for sprinkling
200 g (7 oz) butter, chopped
5 g (¼ cup) sage leaves, torn
2 garlic cloves, crushed
shaved Parmesan cheese,
  to garnish

Drain the beetroot, then grate it into a bowl. Add the Parmesan and ricotta and mix well. Lay a sheet of pasta on a flat surface and place evenly spaced tablespoons of the ricotta mixture on the pasta to give 12 mounds — four across and three down. Flatten the mounds of filling slightly. Lightly brush the edges of the pasta sheet and around each pile of filling with water.

Place a second sheet of pasta over the top and gently press around each mound to seal and enclose the filling. Using a pasta wheel or sharp knife, cut the pasta into 12 ravioli. Lay them out separately on a lined tray that has been sprinkled with cornmeal. Repeat with the remaining filling and lasagne sheets to make 24 ravioli. Gently remove any air bubbles after cutting so that they are completely sealed.

Cook the pasta in a large saucepan of boiling water until *al dente*. Drain, divide among four serving plates and keep warm. Melt the butter in a saucepan and cook for 3–4 minutes, or until golden brown. Remove from the heat, stir in the sage and garlic and spoon over the ravioli. Sprinkle with shaved Parmesan and season with ground pepper.

Serves 4

Pumpkin and feta pie

700 g (1 lb 9 oz) butternut pumpkin
(squash), cut into 2 cm (³/₄ inch)
pieces
4 garlic cloves, unpeeled
5 tablespoons olive oil
2 small red onions, halved and
sliced
1 tablespoon balsamic vinegar
1 tablespoon soft brown sugar
100 g (3¹/₂ oz) good-quality feta
cheese, broken into small pieces
1 tablespoon chopped rosemary
1 large sheet ready-rolled shortcrust
pastry

Preheat the oven to 200°C (400°F/
Gas 6). Place the pumpkin and garlic
cloves on a baking tray, drizzle with
2 tablespoons olive oil and bake for
25–30 minutes, or until the pumpkin
is tender. Transfer the pumpkin to a
large bowl and the garlic to a plate.
Leave the pumpkin to cool.

Meanwhile, heat 2 tablespoons oil in
a pan, add the onion and cook over
medium heat, stirring occasionally,
for 10 minutes. Add the vinegar and
sugar and cook for 15 minutes, or
until the onion is caramelized.
Remove from the heat and add to
the pumpkin. Cool completely.

Add the feta and rosemary to the
pumpkin. Squeeze out the garlic flesh
and mix it through the vegetables.
Season with salt and ground pepper.

Roll out the pastry between two
sheets of baking paper to a 35 cm
(14 inch) circle. Remove the top sheet
of paper and place the bottom paper
with the pastry on a tray. Arrange
the pumpkin and feta mixture on top,
leaving a 4 cm (1¹/₂ inch) border. Fold
over the edges, pleating as you fold,
and bake for 30 minutes, or until crisp
and golden.

Serves 6

Hokkien noodles with Asian greens and glazed tofu

300 g (10½ oz) firm tofu
60 ml (¼ cup) kecap manis
1 tablespoon mushroom soy sauce
1 tablespoon vegetarian oyster sauce
1 teaspoon sesame oil
1 tablespoon peanut oil
2 garlic cloves, crushed
1 tablespoon grated fresh ginger
1 onion, cut into wedges
450 g (1 bunch) choy sum, roughly
  chopped
500 g (1 bunch) baby bok choy
  (pak choi), roughly chopped
450 g (1 lb) fresh hokkien (egg)
  noodles, separated
2 tablespoons peanut oil, extra

Cut the tofu into 1 cm (½ inch) thick slices and place in a shallow, non-metallic dish. Mix together the kecap manis, soy and oyster sauces and pour over the tofu. Leave to marinate for about 15 minutes, then drain and reserve the marinade.

Heat the oils in a wok over medium heat, add the garlic, ginger and onion and stir-fry until the onion is soft. Remove. Add the green vegetables to the wok and stir-fry until just wilted. Remove. Add the separated noodles and the reserved marinade and stir-fry until heated through. Remove from the wok and divide among four plates.

Fry the tofu in the extra oil until it is browned on both sides. Serve the noodles topped with the tofu, green vegetables and onion mixture.

Serves 4

Zucchini, thyme and bocconcini pizza

Pizza base
500 g (4 cups) plain (all-purpose) flour
7 g (1/8 oz) sachet dried yeast
1 teaspoon salt
1 teaspoon sugar
1 tablespoon olive oil

8 zucchini (courgettes), cut into fine rounds
2 teaspoons grated lemon zest
15 g (1/4 cup) finely chopped parsley
2 teaspoons thyme sprigs
4 garlic cloves, crushed
4 tablespoons olive oil
500 g (1 lb 2 oz) bocconcini cheese, finely diced
50 g (1/2 cup) grated Parmesan cheese
1 tablespoon extra virgin olive oil

Preheat the oven to 220°C (425°F/ Gas 7). To make the pizza base, mix together the flour, yeast, salt and sugar in a large bowl, and make a well in the centre. Pour the oil and 310 ml (1 1/4 cups) lukewarm water into the well and mix until the flour is incorporated and a soft dough forms. Turn onto a floured bench and knead for 10 minutes, or until the dough is smooth and elastic. Put the dough in a lightly greased bowl, cover with plastic wrap and leave in a warm place for about 40 minutes, or until doubled in size. Punch the dough down, and knead for 1 minute. Divide in half and roll each half out to 5 mm (1/4 inch) thick. Transfer the bases to two pizza trays.

Place the zucchini rounds, lemon zest, parsley, thyme, garlic and olive oil in a bowl and mix together. Top each pizza base evenly with half the bocconcini and half the Parmesan, then spoon on the zucchini mixture. Evenly distribute the remaining bocconcini and Parmesan over the top, season well with salt and pepper, and drizzle with the extra virgin olive oil. Cook for 15–20 minutes, or until the base is crisp, and the topping is warmed through and golden.

Makes 2

Asparagus and pistachio risotto

1 litre (4 cups) vegetable stock
250 ml (1 cup) white wine
80 ml (1/3 cup) extra virgin olive oil
1 red onion, finely chopped
440 g (2 cups) arborio rice
310 g (10¾ oz) asparagus spears,
   trimmed and cut into 3 cm
   (1¼ inch) pieces
125 ml (½ cup) cream
100 g (1 cup) grated Parmesan
   cheese
40 g (½ cup) shelled pistachio nuts,
   toasted and roughly chopped

Heat the stock and wine in a large saucepan, bring to the boil, then reduce the heat, cover and keep at a low simmer.

Heat the olive oil in another large saucepan. Add the onion and cook over medium heat for 3 minutes, or until soft. Add the rice and stir until the rice is translucent.

Add 125 ml (½ cup) hot stock, stirring constantly over medium heat until the liquid is absorbed. Continue adding more stock, 125 ml (½ cup) at a time, stirring constantly for 20–25 minutes, or until all the stock is absorbed and the rice is tender and creamy. Add the asparagus during the last 5 minutes of cooking. Remove from the heat.

Stand for 2 minutes, then stir in the cream and Parmesan, and season to taste with salt and black pepper. Serve sprinkled with pistachios.

Serves 4–6

Sichuan-style eggplant

Sauce
3 teaspoons chilli paste with garlic
2 tablespoons shao tsing wine
2 tablespoons soy sauce
½ teaspoon sugar
2 teaspoons Chinese black vinegar
250 ml (1 cup) vegetable stock
½ teaspoon sesame oil

2 tablespoons vegetable oil
500 g (1 lb 2 oz) eggplant (aubergine),
    cut into large dice
4 garlic cloves, finely sliced
1 tablespoon julienned ginger
4 spring onions (scallions), finely
    sliced on the diagonal
1 red chilli, finely chopped
steamed jasmine rice, to serve

To make the sauce, combine the chilli paste, shao tsing, soy sauce, sugar, black vinegar, stock and sesame oil with 125 ml (½ cup) water and mix together well.

Heat a wok over high heat, add the vegetable oil, eggplant, garlic, ginger, spring onion and chilli and stir-fry for 3 minutes. Pour in the sauce, then reduce the heat and braise, covered, for 20 minutes, stirring occasionally, until the eggplant is tender and the sauce has been absorbed.

Serve with steamed jasmine rice.

Serves 4

Penne with tomato and onion jam with olives

60 ml (¼ cup) olive oil
4 red onions, sliced
1 tablespoon soft brown sugar
2 tablespoons balsamic vinegar
2 x 400 g (14 oz) tins tomatoes
500 g (1 lb 2 oz) penne rigate
150 g (5½ oz) small pitted black olives or pitted and halved Kalamata olives
75 g (¾ cup) grated Parmesan cheese

Heat the oil in a non-stick frying pan over medium heat. Add the onion and sugar and cook for 25–30 minutes, or until caramelized.

Stir in the vinegar, bring to the boil and cook for 5 minutes. Add the tomatoes, return to the boil, then reduce the heat to medium–low and simmer for 25 minutes, or until the tomatoes are reduced and jam-like.

Cook the pasta in a large saucepan of rapidly boiling salted water according to the packet instructions until *al dente*. Drain, then return to the pan. Add the tomato mixture and olives and stir to combine well. Season to taste with salt and black pepper and garnish with the grated Parmesan.

Serves 4

Notes: Caramelized onions will keep for a few days if covered with oil and stored in the refrigerator. The onions can be combined with goat's cheese to make a quick puff pastry tart or used as a pizza topping.

Bean and capsicum stew

200 g (1 cup) dried haricot beans
2 tablespoons olive oil
2 large garlic cloves, crushed
1 red onion, cut into thin wedges
1 red capsicum (pepper), cut into
   1.5 cm (5/8 inch) cubes
1 green capsicum (pepper), cut into
   1.5 cm (5/8 inch) cubes
2 x 400 g (14 oz) tins chopped
   tomatoes
2 tablespoons tomato paste (purée)
500 ml (2 cups) vegetable stock
2 tablespoons chopped basil
125 g (2/3 cup) Kalamata olives, pitted
1–2 teaspoons soft brown sugar

Put the haricot beans in a large bowl, cover with cold water and soak overnight. Rinse well, then transfer to a saucepan, cover with cold water and cook for 45 minutes, or until just tender. Drain.

Heat the oil in a saucepan. Cook the garlic and onion over medium heat for 2–3 minutes, or until the onion is soft. Add the red and green capsicums and cook for a further 5 minutes.

Stir in the tomato, tomato paste, stock and beans. Simmer, covered, for 40 minutes, or until the beans are cooked through. Stir in the basil, olives and sugar. Season well with salt and pepper before serving.

Serves 4–6

Freeform pumpkin, spinach and ricotta lasagne

60 ml (¼ cup) olive oil
1.5 kg (3 lb 5 oz) butternut pumpkin
   (squash), cut into 1.5 cm (⅝ inch)
   dice
500 g (1 lb 2 oz) English spinach
   leaves, thoroughly washed
4 fresh lasagne sheets (12 x
   20 cm/ 5 x 8 inches)
500 g (2 cups) ricotta cheese
2 tablespoons cream
25 g (¼ cup) grated Parmesan
   cheese
pinch ground nutmeg

Heat the oil in a non-stick frying pan over medium heat. Add the pumpkin and toss. Cook, stirring occasionally, for 15 minutes, or until tender (don't worry if the pumpkin is slightly mashed). Season and keep warm.

Cook the spinach in a large saucepan of boiling water for 30 seconds, or until wilted. Using a slotted spoon, transfer to a bowl of cold water. Drain well and squeeze out as much excess water as possible. Finely chop the spinach. Add the lasagne sheets to the pan of boiling water and cook, stirring occasionally, until *al dente*. Drain and lay the sheets side-by-side on a clean tea towel. Cut each sheet widthways into thirds.

Put the ricotta, cream, Parmesan, spinach and nutmeg in a small pan. Stir over low heat for 2–3 minutes, or until warmed through. Work quickly to assemble. Place a piece of lasagne on the base of each plate. Using half the pumpkin, top each of the sheets, then cover with another piece of lasagne. Use half the ricotta mixture to spread over the lasagne sheets, then add another lasagne piece. Top with the remaining pumpkin, then remaining ricotta mixture. Season well and serve immediately.

Serves 4

Mixed Asian mushrooms with dashi

1 teaspoon dashi granules
1 tablespoon shoyu
1 tablespoon mirin
1½ tablespoons vegetable oil
150 g (5½ oz) oyster mushrooms,
  halved if large
300 g (10½ oz) fresh shiitake
  mushrooms, sliced
300 g (10½ oz) enoki mushrooms,
  separated into small bunches
1 teaspoon finely grated fresh ginger
1 spring onion (scallion), white part
  finely chopped, green part shredded
300 g (10½ oz) shimeji mushrooms,
  separated

In a small bowl or jug, combine the dashi granules with 125 ml (½ cup) boiling water, then stir in the shoyu and mirin. Set aside.

Heat a wok over high heat, add 1 tablespoon oil and swirl to coat. Add the oyster, shiitake and enoki mushrooms in batches and stir-fry for 1–2 minutes, or until wilted and softened.

Heat the remaining oil in the wok, add the ginger and white part of the spring onions and stir-fry for 30 seconds, or until fragrant. Return all the cooked mushrooms to the wok along with the dashi mixture and allow to come to the boil. Stir-fry for an additional minute or until the mushrooms are heated through. Remove from the heat, add the shimeji mushrooms and toss through to wilt with the heat from the other mushrooms. Garnish with the spring onion greens and serve immediately.

Serves 4

Salad pizza

4 ready-made individual thick
   pizza bases
2 tablespoons tomato paste (purée)
2 teaspoons chopped oregano
60 g (2¼ oz) feta cheese, crumbled
100 g (⅔ cup) grated mozzarella
   cheese
60 g (2¼ oz) Parmesan cheese,
   grated
100 g (3½ oz) baby rocket (arugula)
   leaves, trimmed
3 tablespoons flat-leaf (Italian) parsley
¼ small red onion, thinly sliced
60 ml (¼ cup) olive oil
1 tablespoon lemon juice
1 teaspoon Dijon mustard
50 g (1¾ oz) Parmesan cheese,
   extra, shaved

Preheat the oven to 200°C (400°F/
Gas 6). Place the pizza bases on
baking trays. Spread with tomato
paste and sprinkle with oregano,
feta and the grated cheeses. Bake
for 12 minutes, or until bubbling.

Meanwhile, combine the rocket,
parsley and onion in a bowl. Whisk
together the oil, lemon juice and
mustard, and toss through the salad.

Top the pizzas with salad and sprinkle
with shaved Parmesan. Season with
ground pepper and serve immediately.

Serves 4

Green curry with sweet potato and eggplant

1 tablespoon oil
1 onion, chopped
1–2 tablespoons green curry paste
   (see Note)
1 medium eggplant (aubergine),
   quartered and sliced
400 ml (14 fl oz) tin coconut milk
250 ml (1 cup) vegetable stock
6 makrut (kaffir) lime leaves
1 orange sweet potato, cut into
   cubes
2 teaspoons soft brown sugar
2 tablespoons lime juice
2 teaspoons lime zest
coriander (cilantro) leaves,
   to garnish

Heat the oil in a large wok or frying pan. Add the onion and curry paste and cook, stirring, over medium heat for 3 minutes. Add the eggplant and cook for a further 4–5 minutes, or until softened. Pour in the coconut milk and stock, bring to the boil, then reduce the heat and simmer for 5 minutes. Add the lime leaves and sweet potato and cook, stirring occasionally, for 10 minutes, or until the vegetables are very tender.

Mix in the sugar, lime juice and lime zest until well combined with the vegetables. Season to taste with salt. Garnish with fresh coriander leaves and serve with steamed rice.

Serves 4–6

Note: If this is to be a vegetarian meal, make sure you choose a green curry paste that does not contain shrimp paste.

Roasted chunky ratatouille cannelloni

1 medium eggplant (aubergine)
2 zucchini (courgettes)
1 large red capsicum (pepper)
1 large green capsicum (pepper)
3–4 ripe Roma (plum) tomatoes
12 unpeeled garlic cloves
3 tablespoons olive oil
300 ml (10½ fl oz) Italian tomato
  passata
350 g (12 oz) cannelloni tubes
3 tablespoons shredded basil
300 g (10½ oz) ricotta cheese
100 g (3½ oz) feta cheese
1 egg, lightly beaten
50 g (1¾ oz) pecorino pepato
  cheese, grated

Preheat the oven to 200°C (400°F/ Gas 6). Cut the eggplant, zucchini, capsicums and tomatoes into 2 cm (¾ inch) cubes and place in a baking dish with the garlic. Drizzle with the oil and toss to coat. Bake for 1 hour 30 minutes, or until the vegetables are tender and the tomatoes slightly mushy. Peel and lightly mash the garlic cloves.

Pour the passata over the base of a large ovenproof dish. Spoon the ratatouille into the cannelloni tubes and arrange in the dish.

Combine the basil, ricotta, feta and egg, season well and spoon over the cannelloni. Sprinkle with the pecorino and bake for 30 minutes, or until the cannelloni is soft.

Serves 6–8

Tofu, snowpea and mushroom stir-fry

250 g (1¼ cups) jasmine rice
60 ml (¼ cup) peanut oil
600 g (1 lb 5 oz) firm tofu, drained,
   cut into 2 cm (¾ inch) cubes
2 teaspoons sambal oelek or
   chilli paste
2 garlic cloves, finely chopped
400 g (14 oz) fresh Asian mushrooms
   (shiitake, oyster or black fungus),
   sliced
300 g (10½ oz) snowpeas
   (mangetout), trimmed
60 ml (¼ cup) kecap manis

Bring a large saucepan of water to the boil. Add the rice and cook for 12 minutes, stirring occasionally. Drain well.

Meanwhile, heat a wok until very hot. Add 2 tablespoons of the peanut oil and swirl to coat. Add the tofu in two batches and stir-fry on all sides for 2–3 minutes, or until lightly browned. Transfer to a plate.

Heat the remaining oil in the wok, add the sambal oelek, garlic, mushrooms, snowpeas and 1 tablespoon water and stir-fry for 1–2 minutes, or until the vegetables are almost cooked but still crunchy.

Return the tofu to the wok, add the kecap manis and stir-fry for 1 minute, or until heated through and well combined. Serve immediately with the jasmine rice.

Serves 4

Notes: Firm tofu is suitable to stir-fry as it will hold its shape.
As a variation, use 3 teaspoons grated fresh ginger instead of sambal oelek.

Fusilli with broccolini, chilli and olives

3 tablespoons olive oil
1 onion, finely chopped
3 garlic cloves
1 teaspoon chilli flakes
700 g (1 lb 9 oz) broccolini, cut into
  1 cm (1/2 inch) pieces
125 ml (1/2 cup) vegetable stock
400 g (14 oz) fusilli pasta
90 g (1/2 cup) black olives, pitted
  and chopped
7 g (1/4 cup) finely chopped parsley
25 g (1/4 cup) grated Pecorino cheese
2 tablespoons basil leaves, shredded

Heat the olive oil in a large non-stick frying pan over medium heat. Cook the onion, garlic and chilli until softened, then add the broccolini and cook for 5 minutes. Pour in the stock and cook, covered, for 5 minutes.

Meanwhile, cook the fusilli in a large saucepan of rapidly boiling water until *al dente*. Drain and keep warm.

When the broccolini is tender, remove from the heat. Add to the pasta with the olives, parsley, Pecorino and basil, and season well. Gently toss together and serve immediately.

Serves 4

Rustic Greek pie

450 g (1 lb) packet frozen spinach,
  thawed
1 large sheet ready-rolled shortcrust
  pastry, thawed
3 garlic cloves, finely chopped
150 g (5½ oz) haloumi cheese,
  grated
120 g (4½ oz) feta cheese,
  crumbled
1 tablespoon oregano sprigs
2 eggs
60 ml (¼ cup) cream
lemon wedges, to serve

Preheat the oven to 210°C (415°F/
Gas 6–7). Squeeze the excess liquid
from the spinach.

Place the pastry on a baking tray
and spread the spinach in the middle,
leaving a 3 cm (1¼ inch) border
around the edge. Sprinkle the garlic
over the spinach and pile the haloumi
and feta on top. Sprinkle with oregano
and season well. Cut a short slit into
each corner of the pastry, then tuck
each side of pastry over to form a
border around the filling.

Lightly beat the eggs with the cream
and carefully pour the egg mixture
over the spinach filling. Bake for
30–40 minutes, or until the pastry is
golden and the filling is set. Serve
with the lemon wedges.

Serves 4

Sweet ginger and chilli vegetables with rice noodles

500 g (1 lb 2 oz) fresh rice noodle
  sheets, at room temperature
2 tablespoons oil
1 teaspoon sesame oil
3 tablespoons grated fresh ginger
1 onion, thinly sliced
1 red capsicum (pepper), sliced
100 g (3½ oz) fresh shiitake
  mushrooms, sliced
200 g (7 oz) baby corn, halved
500 g (1 lb 2 oz) Chinese broccoli
  (gai larn), sliced
200 g (7 oz) snowpeas (mangetout)
3 tablespoons sweet chilli sauce
2 tablespoons light soy sauce
2 tablespoons dark soy sauce
1 tablespoon lime juice
16 Thai basil leaves

Cut the noodle sheets into 3 cm (1¼ inch) wide strips, then cut each strip into three. Gently separate the noodles (you may need to run a little cold water over them to do this).

Heat the oils in a wok, add the ginger and onion and stir-fry until the onion is soft. Add the vegetables and stir-fry until brightly coloured and just tender.

Add the noodles to the vegetables and stir-fry until the noodles start to soften. Stir in the combined sauces and lime juice and cook until heated through. Remove from the heat, toss through the basil leaves and serve.

Serves 4

Zucchini pasta bake

200 g (7 oz) risoni
40 g (1½ oz) butter
4 spring onions (scallions), thinly
  sliced
400 g (14 oz) zucchini (courgettes),
  grated
4 eggs
125 ml (½ cup) cream
100 g (3½ oz) ricotta cheese
  (see Note)
100 g (²/₃ cup) grated mozzarella
  cheese
75 g (¾ cup) grated Parmesan
  cheese

Preheat the oven to 180°C (350°F/
Gas 4). Cook the pasta in a large
saucepan of rapidly boiling water until
al dente. Drain well.

Meanwhile, heat the butter in a frying
pan, add the spring onion and cook
for 1 minute, then add the zucchini
and cook for a further 4 minutes, or
until soft. Cool slightly.

Combine the eggs, cream, ricotta,
mozzarella, risoni and half of the
Parmesan, then stir in the zucchini
mixture. Season well. Spoon into four
500 ml (2 cup) greased ovenproof
dishes, but not to the brim. Sprinkle
with the remaining Parmesan and
cook for 25–30 minutes, or until firm
and golden.

Serves 4

Note: With such simple flavours, it is
important to use good-quality fresh
ricotta from the delicatessen or the
deli section of your local supermarket.

Eggplant and mushroom skewers with tomato concassé

12 long rosemary sprigs
18 Swiss brown mushrooms
1 small eggplant (aubergine),
 cut into 2 cm (³/₄ inch) cubes
60 ml (¼ cup) olive oil
2 tablespoons balsamic vinegar
2 garlic cloves, crushed
1 teaspoon sugar
olive oil, for brushing
sea salt, to sprinkle (optional)

Tomato concassé
5 tomatoes
1 tablespoon olive oil
1 small onion, finely chopped
1 garlic clove, crushed
1 tablespoon tomato paste (purée)
2 teaspoons sugar
2 teaspoons balsamic vinegar
1 tablespoon chopped flat-leaf
 (Italian) parsley

Remove the leaves from the rosemary sprigs, leaving 5 cm (2 inches) on the tip. Reserve 1 tablespoon of the leaves. Cut the mushrooms in half, stems intact. Place the mushrooms and eggplant in a non-metallic bowl. Pour on the combined oil, vinegar, garlic and sugar, then season and toss. Marinate for 15 minutes.

Score a cross in the base of each tomato. Put in a bowl of boiling water for 30 seconds then plunge into cold water. Peel the skin away from the cross. Cut in half and scoop out the seeds with a teaspoon. Dice. Heat the oil in a saucepan over medium heat. Cook the onion and garlic for 2–3 minutes, or until soft. Reduce the heat and add the tomato, tomato paste, sugar, vinegar and parsley. Simmer for 10 minutes, or until the liquid has evaporated. Keep warm.

Thread alternating mushroom and eggplant pieces onto the rosemary sprigs (3 mushroom halves and 2 cubes of eggplant on each). Lightly oil a chargrill pan (griddle) or barbecue hotplate and cook the skewers for 7–8 minutes, or until the eggplant is tender, turning occasionally. Serve with concassé and sprinkle with salt and rosemary.

Serves 4

Soya bean moussaka

2 eggplants (aubergines)
1 tablespoon oil
1 onion, finely chopped
2 garlic cloves, crushed
2 ripe tomatoes, peeled, seeded
  and chopped
2 teaspoons tomato paste (purée)
½ teaspoon dried oregano
125 ml (½ cup) dry white wine
300 g (10½ oz) tin soya beans,
  rinsed and drained
3 tablespoons chopped flat-leaf
  (Italian) parsley
30 g (1 oz) butter
2 tablespoons plain (all-purpose)
  flour
pinch ground nutmeg
315 ml (1¼ cups) milk
40 g (⅓ cup) grated Cheddar
  cheese

Preheat the oven to 180°C (350°F/ Gas 4). Cut the eggplants in half lengthways. Spoon out the flesh, leaving a 1.5 cm (⅝ inch) border and place on a large baking tray, cut-side up. Use crumpled foil around the sides of the eggplant to support it.

Heat the oil in a frying pan. Cook the onion and garlic over medium heat for 3 minutes, or until soft. Add the tomato, tomato paste, oregano and wine. Bring to the boil and cook for 3 minutes, or until the liquid is reduced and the tomato soft. Stir in the soya beans and parsley.

To make the sauce, melt the butter in a saucepan. Stir in the flour and cook over medium heat for 1 minute, or until pale and foamy. Remove from the heat and gradually stir in the nutmeg and milk. Return to the heat and stir constantly until the sauce boils and thickens. Pour one-third of the white sauce into the tomato mixture and stir well.

Spoon the mixture into the eggplant shells. Smooth the surface before spreading the remaining sauce evenly over the top and sprinkling with cheese. Bake for 50 minutes, or until cooked through. Serve hot.

Serves 4

Conchiglie rigate with spring vegetables

500 g (1 lb 2 oz) conchiglie rigate
310 g (2 cups) frozen peas
310 g (2 cups) frozen broad (fava) beans, blanched and peeled
80 ml (⅓ cup) olive oil
6 spring onions (scallions), cut into 3 cm (1¼ inch) pieces
2 garlic cloves, finely chopped
250 ml (1 cup) vegetable or chicken stock, preferably home-made
12 thin fresh asparagus spears, cut into 5 cm (2 inch) lengths
½ teaspoon finely grated lemon zest
60 ml (¼ cup) lemon juice
shaved Parmesan cheese, to garnish

Cook the pasta in a large saucepan of boiling water until *al dente*. Drain, then return to the pan. Meanwhile, place the peas in a saucepan of boiling water and cook them for 1–2 minutes, or until tender. Remove with a slotted spoon and plunge into cold water. Add the broad beans to the same saucepan of boiling water and cook for 1–2 minutes, then drain and plunge into cold water. Remove and slip the skins off.

Heat 2 tablespoons of the oil in a frying pan. Add the spring onion and garlic and cook over medium heat for 2 minutes, or until softened. Pour in the stock and cook for 5 minutes, or until slightly reduced. Add the asparagus and cook for 3–4 minutes, or until bright green and just tender. Stir in the peas and broad beans and cook for 2–3 minutes, or until heated through.

Toss the remaining oil through the pasta, then add the vegetables, lemon zest and lemon juice. Season and toss together well. Serve topped with shaved Parmesan.

Serves 4

Orange sweet potato, spinach and water chestnut stir-fry

300 g (1 1/2 cups) long-grain rice
500 g (1 lb 2 oz) orange sweet
  potato
1 tablespoon oil
2 garlic cloves, crushed
2 teaspoons sambal oelek
  (see Notes)
225 g (8 oz) tin water chestnuts,
  sliced
2 teaspoons grated palm sugar
  (see Notes)
400 g (14 oz) English spinach,
  stems removed
2 tablespoons soy sauce
2 tablespoons vegetable stock

Bring a large saucepan of water to the boil. Add the rice and cook for 12 minutes, stirring occasionally. Drain well.

Meanwhile, cut the sweet potato into 1.5 cm x 1.5 cm ($5/8$ inch x $5/8$ inch) cubes and cook in a large saucepan of boiling water for 15 minutes, or until tender. Drain well.

Heat a wok until very hot, add the oil and swirl to coat. Stir-fry the garlic and sambal oelek for 1 minute, or until fragrant. Add the sweet potato and water chestnuts and stir-fry over medium–high heat for 2 minutes. Reduce the heat to medium, add the palm sugar and cook for a further 2 minutes, or until the sugar has melted. Add the spinach, soy sauce and stock and toss until the spinach has just wilted. Serve on a bed of steamed rice.

Serves 4

Notes: Sambal oelek is made from mashed fresh red chillies mixed with salt and vinegar or tamarind.
Palm sugar is available from most large supermarkets in jars or wrapped in paper. Use demerara or soft brown sugar if not available.

Mushroom pot pies

5 tablespoons olive oil
1 leek, sliced
1 garlic clove, crushed
1 kg (2 lb 4 oz) large field
  mushrooms, roughly chopped
1 teaspoon chopped thyme
300 ml (10½ fl oz) cream
1 sheet ready-rolled puff pastry,
  thawed
1 egg yolk, beaten, to glaze

Preheat the oven to 180°C (350°F/ Gas 4). Heat 1 tablespoon of the oil in a frying pan over medium heat. Cook the leek and garlic for 5 minutes, or until the leek is soft and translucent. Transfer to a large saucepan.

Heat the remaining oil in the frying pan over high heat and cook the mushrooms in two batches, stirring frequently, for 5–7 minutes per batch, or until the mushrooms have released their juices and are soft and slightly coloured. Transfer to the saucepan, then add the thyme.

Place the saucepan over high heat and stir in the cream. Cook, stirring occasionally, for 7–8 minutes, or until the cream has reduced to a thick sauce. Remove from the heat and season well with salt and pepper.

Divide the filling among four 315 ml (1¼ cup) ramekins or ovenproof bowls. Cut the pastry into rounds slightly larger than each dish. Brush the rim of the ramekins with a little of the egg yolk, place the pastry on top and press down to seal. Brush the top with the remaining egg yolk. Place the ramekins on a metal tray. Bake for 20–25 minutes, or until the pastry has risen and is golden brown.

Serves 4

Fusilli with roasted tomatoes, tapenade and bocconcini

800 g (1 lb 12 oz) cherry or teardrop
   tomatoes (or a mixture of both),
   halved if they are large
500 g (1 lb 2 oz) fusilli
300 g (10½ oz) baby bocconcini
   cheese, sliced
1 tablespoon chopped thyme

Tapenade
1½ tablespoons capers
2 small garlic cloves
185 g (1½ cups) sliced black
   olives
3 tablespoons lemon juice
4–5 tablespoons extra virgin
   olive oil

Preheat the oven to 200°C (400°F/
Gas 6). Place the tomatoes on a
baking tray, sprinkle with salt and
pepper and bake for 10 minutes,
or until slightly dried.

To make the tapenade, place the
capers, garlic, olives and lemon juice
in a food processor and mix together.
With the motor running, gradually
add the oil until the mixture forms
a smooth paste.

Cook the pasta in a large saucepan
of rapidly boiling water until *al dente*,
then drain.

Toss the tapenade and bocconcini
through the hot pasta. Top with the
roasted tomatoes and thyme and
serve immediately.

Serves 4–6

Rice and red lentil pilau

Garam masala
1 tablespoon coriander seeds
1 tablespoon cardamom pods
1 tablespoon cumin seeds
1 teaspoon whole black peppercorns
1 teaspoon whole cloves
1 small cinnamon stick, crushed

60 ml (¼ cup) oil
1 onion, chopped
3 garlic cloves, chopped
200 g (1 cup) basmati rice
250 g (1 cup) red lentils
750 ml (3 cups) hot vegetable stock
spring onions (scallions), sliced on
   the diagonal, to garnish

To make the garam masala, place all the spices in a dry frying pan and shake over medium heat for 1 minute, or until fragrant. Blend in a spice grinder or blender to a fine powder.

Heat the oil in a saucepan. Add the onion, garlic and 3 teaspoons garam masala. Cook over medium heat for 3 minutes, or until the onion is soft.

Stir in the rice and lentils and cook for 2 minutes. Add the stock and stir well. Slowly bring to the boil, then reduce the heat and simmer, covered, for 15–20 minutes, or until the rice is cooked and all the stock has been absorbed. Gently fluff the rice with a fork. Garnish with spring onion.

Serves 4–6

Note: If you prefer, you can use ready-made garam masala instead of making it.

Tamari roasted almonds with spicy green beans

3 tablespoons sesame oil
500 g (2½ cups) jasmine rice
1 long red chilli, seeded and
  finely chopped
2 cm (¾ inch) piece ginger, peeled
  and grated
2 garlic cloves, crushed
375 g (13 oz) green beans, cut into
  5 cm (2 inch) lengths
125 ml (½ cup) hoisin sauce
1 tablespoon soft brown sugar
2 tablespoons mirin
125 g (4½ oz) tamari roasted
  almonds, roughly chopped
  (see Note)

Preheat the oven to 200°C (400°F/ Gas 6). Heat 1 tablespoon of oil in a 1.5 litre (6 cup) ovenproof dish, add the rice and stir until well coated. Stir in 1 litre (4 cups) boiling water. Cover and bake for 20 minutes, or until all the water is absorbed. Keep warm.

Meanwhile, heat the remaining oil in a wok or large frying pan and cook the chilli, ginger and garlic for 1 minute, or until lightly browned. Add the beans, hoisin sauce and sugar and stir-fry for 2 minutes. Stir in the mirin and cook for 1 minute, or until the beans are tender but still crunchy.

Remove from the heat and stir in the almonds just before serving. Serve with the rice.

Serves 4–6

Note: Tamari roasted almonds are available from health-food stores. If unavailable, soak unpeeled almonds in tamari for 30 minutes. Drain and dry with paper towels. Heat a non-stick frying pan with 1 tablespoon oil. Toss the almonds for 2–3 minutes, then drain.

Somen nests with eggplant and shiitake mushrooms

2 small eggplants (aubergines),
    cut into 1 cm (½ inch) thick slices
12 dried shiitake mushrooms
60 ml (¼ cup) vegetable oil
100 g (3½ oz) fresh enoki
    mushrooms
1 teaspoon dashi granules
1 tablespoon sugar
1 tablespoon white miso
1 tablespoon mirin (sweet rice wine)
60 ml (¼ cup) Japanese soy sauce
320 g (11 oz) dried somen noodles

Blanch the eggplant in boiling water for 5 minutes. Drain, transfer to a plate and weigh down for 15 minutes to press out any remaining liquid. Pat dry.

Soak the dried shiitake mushrooms in 250 ml (1 cup) boiling water for 10 minutes. Drain and reserve the liquid. Heat the oil in a large frying pan and cook the eggplant slices in batches until golden brown on both sides. Remove. Add the enoki mushrooms and cook for 10 seconds. Remove. Stir in the dashi, sugar, miso, mirin, soy sauce, reserved mushroom liquid, shiitake mushrooms and 125 ml (½ cup) water. Bring to the boil, then cover and simmer for 10 minutes.

Cook the somen noodles in boiling water for 3 minutes, or until tender. Drain well.

Place nests of the noodles onto plates, top with eggplant slices and the mushrooms and drizzle with the sauce. Serve immediately.

Serves 4

Conchiglie stuffed with roast pumpkin and ricotta

1 kg (2 lb 4 oz) butternut pumpkin
  (squash), cut into large wedges
olive oil, to drizzle
10 unpeeled garlic cloves
500 g (1 lb 2 oz) ricotta cheese
20 g (1/3 cup) finely shredded basil
750 ml (3 cups) bottled Italian pasta
  sauce (pomodoro)
125 ml (1/2 cup) dry white wine
56 conchiglie (or 32 giant conchiglie)
100 g (1 cup) grated Parmesan
  cheese

Preheat the oven to 200°C (400°F/ Gas 6). Place the pumpkin in a baking dish, drizzle with olive oil and season. Bake for 30 minutes, then add the garlic and bake for 15 minutes, or until tender. Cool slightly, then peel and mash the pumpkin and garlic. Mix with the ricotta and half the basil and season to taste.

Put the pasta sauce and wine in a saucepan, bring to the boil, then reduce the heat and simmer for 10 minutes, or until slightly thickened.

Cook the pasta in rapidly boiling water until *al dente*. Lay out on a tea towel to dry, then fill with the pumpkin mixture. Spread any remaining filling in a large ovenproof dish, top with the shells and pour on the sauce. Sprinkle with Parmesan and the remaining basil and bake for about 15–20 minutes (or 30 minutes for the giant shells).

Serves 6

Spaghetti with lemon and rocket

375 g (13 oz) spaghetti
100 g (3½ oz) rocket (arugula),
  finely shredded
1 tablespoon finely chopped
  lemon zest
1 garlic clove, finely chopped
1 small red chilli, seeded and
  finely chopped
1 teaspoon chilli oil
5 tablespoons extra virgin olive oil
60 g (2¼ oz) Parmesan cheese,
  finely grated

Cook the spaghetti according to the packet instructions until *al dente*. Drain well.

Combine the rocket, lemon zest, garlic, chilli, chilli oil, extra virgin olive oil and two-thirds of the grated Parmesan in a large bowl and mix together gently.

Add the pasta to the rocket and lemon mixture and stir together well. Serve topped with the remaining Parmesan and season to taste with salt and cracked black pepper.

Serves 4

Note: If you prefer, you can substitute basil leaves for the rocket.

Green stir-fry with sesame and soy

2 tablespoons light soy sauce
1 tablespoon hoisin sauce
1 tablespoon vegetable or chicken
   stock
2 tablespoons vegetable oil
1 teaspoon sesame oil
4 garlic cloves, finely sliced
2 teaspoons julienned ginger
2 kg (4 bunches) baby bok choy
   (pak choi), cut into quarters,
   well washed and drained
200 g (7 oz) snowpeas (mangetout),
   trimmed
200 g (7 oz) sugar snap peas,
   trimmed
2 tablespoons bamboo shoots,
   julienned
jasmine rice, to serve

In a small jug mix together the light soy sauce, hoisin sauce and stock.

Heat a wok over high heat and add the vegetable and sesame oils. Stir-fry the garlic, ginger and bok choy for 3 minutes. Add the snowpeas, sugar snap peas and bamboo shoots and stir-fry for a further 5 minutes. Pour in the sauce, and gently toss until the sauce has reduced slightly to coat the just tender vegetables. Serve immediately with jasmine rice.

Serves 4

Potato and zucchini casserole

1 large red capsicum (pepper)
60 ml (¼ cup) olive oil
2 onions, sliced
2 garlic cloves, crushed
400 g (14 oz) zucchini (courgettes),
  thickly sliced
400 g (14 oz) small waxy potatoes
  (pontiac, kipfler, desiree), unpeeled,
  cut into 1 cm (½ inch) slices
1 kg (2 lb 4 oz) ripe tomatoes, peeled
  and roughly chopped
1 teaspoon dried oregano
2 tablespoons chopped flat-leaf
  (Italian) parsley
2 tablespoons chopped dill
½ teaspoon ground cinnamon

Preheat the oven to 180°C (350°F/ Gas 4). Remove the seeds and membrane from the red capsicum and cut the flesh into squares.

Heat 2 tablespoons of the olive oil in a heavy-based frying pan over medium heat. Cook the onion, stirring frequently, for 10 minutes. Add the garlic and cook for another 2 minutes. Place all the other ingredients in a large bowl and season generously with salt and pepper. Add the softened onion and garlic and toss everything together. Transfer to a large baking dish and drizzle the remaining oil over the vegetables.

Cover and bake for 1–1½ hours, or until the vegetables are tender, stirring every 30 minutes. Check for doneness by inserting the point of a small knife into the potatoes. When the knife comes away easily, the potato is cooked.

Serves 4–6

Pearl barley and Asian mushroom pilaf

330 g (1½ cups) pearl barley
3 dried shiitake mushrooms
625 ml (2½ cups) vegetable or
  chicken stock
125 ml (½ cup) dry sherry
2 tablespoons olive oil
1 large onion, finely chopped
3 garlic cloves, crushed
2 tablespoons grated fresh ginger
1 teaspoon Sichuan peppercorns,
  crushed
500 g (1 lb 2 oz) mixed fresh
  Asian mushrooms (oyster,
  Swiss brown, enoki)
375 g (13 oz) choy sum, cut into
  short lengths
3 teaspoons kecap manis
1 teaspoon sesame oil

Soak the pearl barley in enough cold water to cover for at least 6 hours, or preferably overnight. Drain.

Soak the shiitake mushrooms in enough boiling water to cover for 15 minutes. Strain, reserving 125 ml (½ cup) of the liquid. Discard the stalks and finely slice the caps.

Heat the stock and sherry in a small saucepan. Cover and keep at a low simmer.

Heat the oil in a large saucepan over medium heat. Cook the onion for 4–5 minutes, or until softened. Add the garlic, ginger and peppercorns and cook for 1 minute. Slice the Asian mushrooms, reserving the enoki for later. Increase the heat and add the mushrooms. Cook for 5 minutes, or until the mushrooms have softened. Add the barley, shiitake mushrooms, reserved soaking liquid and hot stock. Stir well to combine. Bring to the boil, then reduce the heat to low and simmer, covered, for 35 minutes, or until the liquid evaporates.

Steam the choy sum until just wilted. Add to the barley mixture with the enoki mushrooms. Stir in the kecap manis and sesame oil and serve.

Serves 4

Balsamic capsicum on angel hair

300 g (10½ oz) angel hair pasta
2 red capsicums (peppers)
2 yellow capsicums (peppers)
2 green capsicums (peppers)
4 garlic cloves, crushed
2 tablespoons orange juice
80 ml (⅓ cup) balsamic vinegar
100 g (3½ oz) goat's cheese
15 g (½ cup) basil

Cook the pasta in a large saucepan of rapidly boiling water until *al dente*. Drain well.

Cut the capsicums into large flat pieces and place under a hot grill (broiler) until the skins blister and blacken. Leave to cool in a plastic bag, then peel away the skin and cut the flesh into thin strips.

Combine the capsicum strips, garlic, orange juice and balsamic vinegar. Drizzle over the pasta and gently toss.

Serve topped with crumbled goat's cheese and basil and a sprinkling of cracked black pepper.

Serves 4

Vegetable pasta torte

4 small Roma (plum) tomatoes
300 g (10½ oz) orange sweet potato,
  peeled and cut into large chunks
1 red capsicum (pepper)
3 tablespoons oil
200 g (7 oz) fettucine
6 eggs, lightly beaten
250 ml (1 cup) milk
125 g (1 cup) grated Cheddar
  cheese
10 g (½ cup) flat-leaf (Italian)
  parsley leaves
200 g (7 oz) feta cheese, cut
  into large cubes

Preheat the oven to 200°C (400°F/ Gas 6). Place the tomatoes, sweet potato and capsicum in a baking dish, drizzle with oil and season well. Bake for 40 minutes, or until tender.

Peel the capsicum and cut it into large chunks.

Cook the pasta in rapidly boiling water until *al dente*, then drain well. Combine the egg, milk and Cheddar.

Arrange half the vegetables and half the parsley in a greased 24 cm (10 inch) non-stick deep frying pan. Top with half the pasta and feta, then layer with the remaining vegetables, parsley, pasta and feta. Top with the egg mix. Cook over medium heat for 15–20 minutes, or until just set (be careful not to burn the base). Cook under a grill (broiler) for a further 15–20 minutes, or until the top is golden brown. Leave for 5 minutes before turning out to serve.

Serves 6–8

Yellow curry of pumpkin with green beans and cashew nuts

500 ml (2 cups) coconut cream
  (do not shake the can)
3 teaspoons yellow curry paste
125 ml (1/2 cup) vegetable or
  chicken stock
500 g (1 lb 2 oz) Jap pumpkin,
  peeled and diced
300 g (10 1/2 oz) green beans,
  trimmed and cut in half
2 tablespoons soy sauce
2 tablespoons lime juice
1 tablespoon grated palm sugar
7 g (1/4 cup) coriander (cilantro) leaves
40 g (1/4 cup) cashew nuts, toasted
steamed jasmine rice, to serve

Spoon the thick coconut cream from the top of the tin into the wok, and heat until boiling. Add the curry paste, then reduce the heat and simmer, stirring, for 5 minutes, until the oil begins to separate.

Add the remaining coconut cream, stock and pumpkin, and simmer for 10 minutes. Add the green beans and cook for a further 8 minutes, or until the vegetables are tender.

Gently stir in the soy sauce, lime juice, and palm sugar. Garnish with the coriander leaves and cashew nuts and serve with steamed jasmine rice.

Serves 4

Sweet potato and sage risotto

50 ml (1¾ fl oz) extra virgin olive oil
1 red onion, cut into thin wedges
600 g (1 lb 5 oz) orange sweet
    potato, peeled and cut into
    2 cm (¾ inch) cubes
440 g (2 cups) arborio rice
1.25 litres (5 cups) hot vegetable
    stock
75 g (¾ cup) shredded Parmesan
    cheese
3 tablespoons shredded sage
shaved Parmesan cheese, extra,
    to garnish

Heat 3 tablespoons oil in a large saucepan and cook the onion over medium heat for 2–3 minutes, or until softened. Add the sweet potato and rice and stir until well coated in the oil.

Add 125 ml (½ cup) hot stock, stirring constantly over medium heat until the liquid is absorbed. Continue adding more stock, 125 ml (½ cup) at a time, stirring constantly for 20–25 minutes, or until all the stock is absorbed, the sweet potato is cooked and the rice is tender and creamy.

Add the Parmesan and 2 tablespoons of the sage. Season well and stir to combine. Spoon into four bowls and drizzle with the remaining oil. Sprinkle the remaining sage over the top and garnish with shaved Parmesan.

Serves 4

Orecchiette with broccoli

750 g (1 lb 10 oz) broccoli,
  cut into florets
450 g (1 lb) orecchiette
60 ml (¼ cup) extra virgin olive oil
½ teaspoon dried chilli flakes
30 g (⅓ cup) grated Pecorino or
  Parmesan cheese

Blanch the broccoli in a saucepan of boiling salted water for 5 minutes, or until just tender. Remove with a slotted spoon, drain well and return the water to the boil. Cook the pasta in the boiling water until *al dente*, then drain well and return to the pan.

Meanwhile, heat the oil in a heavy-based frying pan and add the chilli flakes and broccoli. Increase the heat to medium and cook, stirring, for 5 minutes, or until the broccoli is well coated and beginning to break apart. Season. Add to the pasta, toss in the cheese and serve.

Serves 6

Balti eggplant and tofu stir-fry

2 tablespoons oil
1 onion, finely chopped
70 g (¼ cup) balti curry paste
300 g (10½ oz) slender eggplant
    (aubergine), cut diagonally into
    1 cm (½ inch) slices
300 g (10½ oz) firm tofu, cut into
    1.5 cm (⅝ inch) cubes
3 ripe tomatoes, cut into wedges
60 ml (¼ cup) vegetable stock
75 g (2½ oz) baby English spinach
    leaves
50 g (⅓ cup) toasted cashews
saffron rice, to serve

Heat a wok or deep frying pan until very hot. Add the oil and swirl to coat. Add the onion and stir-fry over high heat for 3–4 minutes, or until softened and golden.

Stir in the balti curry paste and cook for 1 minute. Add the eggplant and cook for 5 minutes. Stir in the tofu, gently tossing for 3–4 minutes, or until golden.

Add the tomato and stock and cook for 3 minutes, or until the tomato is soft. Stir in the spinach and cook for 1–2 minutes, or until wilted. Season. Sprinkle the cashews over the top and serve with saffron rice.

Serves 4

Mushroom long-life noodles

400 g (14 oz) pancit canton noodles
1 tablespoon peanut oil
3 tablespoons soy sauce
1½ tablespoons mushroom soy
  sauce
1 teaspoon sesame oil
1 teaspoon sugar
250 ml (1 cup) vegetable stock
1 tablespoon grated fresh ginger
2 garlic cloves, crushed
250 g (9 oz) shiitake mushrooms,
  sliced
250 g (9 oz) shimeji mushrooms,
  separated
125 g (4½ oz) wood ear fungus,
  sliced
250 g (9 oz) enoki mushrooms,
  separated
30 g (½ cup) spring onions (scallions),
  finely sliced on the diagonal

Bring a saucepan of water to the boil, and cook the noodles for 3 minutes. Drain, rinse the noodles under cold water, and then drain them once again. Toss the noodles with 1 teaspoon of peanut oil.

In a small bowl, thoroughly mix together the soy sauce, mushroom soy sauce, sesame oil, sugar and vegetable stock.

In a wok, heat the remaining peanut oil over high heat, add the ginger and garlic and stir-fry for 1 minute. Add the shiitake mushrooms, shimeji mushrooms and wood ear fungus and stir-fry for 3 minutes. Add the noodles, enoki mushrooms, spring onion and combined sauce ingredients. Gently toss, cooking until the noodles have absorbed the sauce.

Serves 4

Fettucine with creamy spinach and roast tomato

6 Roma (plum) tomatoes
40 g (1 1/2 oz) butter
2 garlic cloves, crushed
1 onion, chopped
500 g (1 lb 2 oz) English spinach, trimmed
250 ml (1 cup) vegetable stock
125 ml (1/2 cup) thick (double/heavy) cream
500 g (1 lb 2 oz) fresh spinach fettucine
50 g (1 3/4 oz) shaved Parmesan cheese

Preheat the oven to 220°C (425°F/Gas 7). Cut the tomatoes in half lengthways, then cut each half into three wedges. Place the wedges on a lightly greased baking tray and bake for 30–35 minutes, or until softened and slightly golden.

Meanwhile, heat the butter in a large frying pan. Add the garlic and onion and cook over medium heat for 5 minutes, or until the onion is soft. Add the spinach, stock and cream, increase the heat to high and bring to the boil. Simmer rapidly for 5 minutes.

While the spinach mixture is cooking, cook the pasta in a large saucepan of boiling water until *al dente*. Drain and return to the pan. Remove the spinach mixture from the heat and season well. Cool slightly, then process in a food processor until smooth. Toss through the pasta until well coated. Divide among serving bowls, top with the roasted tomatoes and Parmesan shavings, and serve.

Serves 4–6

Italian zucchini pie

600 g (1 lb 5 oz) zucchini (courgettes), grated and mixed with ¼ teaspoon salt
150 g (5½ oz) provolone cheese, grated
120 g (4½ oz) ricotta cheese
3 eggs
2 garlic cloves, crushed
2 teaspoons finely chopped basil
pinch ground nutmeg
2 sheets ready-rolled shortcrust pastry
1 egg (extra), lightly beaten

Preheat the oven to 200°C (400°F/ Gas 6) and heat a baking tray. Grease a 23 cm (9 inch) (top) pie dish. Drain the zucchini in a colander for 30 minutes, then squeeze out any excess liquid. Place in a bowl with the cheeses, eggs, garlic, basil and nutmeg. Season and mix well.

Using two-thirds of the pastry, line the base and sides of the dish. Spoon the filling into the pastry shell and level the surface. Brush the exposed rim of the pastry with egg. Use two-thirds of the remaining pastry to make a lid. Cover the filling with it, pressing the edges together firmly. Trim the edges and reserve the scraps. Crimp the rim. Prick the top all over with a skewer and brush with egg.

From the remaining pastry, cut a strip about 30 cm x 10 cm (12 inches x 4 inches). Cut this into nine lengths 1 cm (½ inch) wide. Press three ropes together at one end and press onto the workbench. Plait the ropes. Make two more plaits, trim the ends and space the plaits parallel across the centre of the pie. Brush with egg. Bake on the hot tray for 50 minutes, or until golden.

Serves 6

Sweet potato ravioli

500 g (1 lb 2 oz) orange sweet
potato, chopped
2 teaspoons lemon juice
190 g (6½ oz) butter
50 g (½ cup) grated Parmesan
cheese
1 tablespoon chopped chives
1 egg, lightly beaten
250 g (9 oz) packet won ton wrappers
2 tablespoons sage, torn
2 tablespoons chopped walnuts

Cook the sweet potato and lemon juice in boiling water for 15 minutes, or until tender. Drain and pat dry with paper towels. Cool for 5 minutes.

Blend the sweet potato and 30 g (1 oz) of the butter in a food processor until smooth. Add the Parmesan, chives and half the egg. Season with salt and freshly ground pepper, and allow to cool completely.

Put 2 teaspoons of the mixture in the centre of half the won ton wrappers. Brush the edges with the remaining egg, then cover with the remaining wrappers. Press the edges firmly to seal. Using a 7 cm (2¾ inch) cutter, cut the ravioli into circles.

Melt the remaining butter in a small saucepan over low heat and cook until golden brown. Remove from the heat.

Cook the ravioli in batches in a large saucepan of boiling water for about 4 minutes. Drain carefully and divide among heated serving plates. Serve the ravioli immediately, drizzled with the butter and sprinkled with the sage and walnuts.

Serves 4

Grilled polenta with shaved fennel salad

500 ml (2 cups) milk
175 g (6 oz) polenta
35 g (⅓ cup) grated Parmesan
  cheese
1 tablespoon butter
200 g (7 oz) fennel bulb
60 g (2 cups) picked watercress
  leaves
1 tablespoon lemon juice
2 tablespoons olive oil
2 tablespoons shaved Parmesan
  cheese

In a heavy-based saucepan, bring the milk and 500 ml (2 cups) water to the boil. Add the polenta, and whisk until thoroughly mixed. Reduce the heat as low as possible and simmer for 40 minutes, stirring occasionally to prevent it sticking. Remove from the heat, stir in the Parmesan and butter and season well. Pour into a greased tray to set (it should be about 2 cm (¾ inch) thick). When cold, cut into six wedges, brush with a little olive oil, and cook in a hot chargrill pan (griddle) or on a barbecue hotplate until crisp brown grill marks appear.

Slice the fennel as thinly as possible and chop the fronds. Toss in a bowl with the watercress, lemon juice, oil and half the shaved Parmesan. Season with salt and black pepper.

Serve the chargrilled polenta with the fennel salad piled to one side, and the remaining shaved Parmesan on top.

Serves 6

Quick mushrooms with red curry sauce

500 ml (2 cups) coconut cream
2 teaspoons red curry paste
  (see Note)
2 teaspoons finely chopped lemon
  grass, white part only
125 ml (½ cup) vegetable stock
250 ml (1 cup) coconut milk
2 teaspoons mushroom soy sauce
1½ tablespoons shaved palm sugar
3 fresh makrut (kaffir) lime leaves
1 tablespoon lime juice
400 g (14 oz) assorted mushrooms
  (shiitake, oyster, enoki, button)
2 tablespoons coriander (cilantro)
  leaves
3 tablespoons torn Thai basil

Place the coconut cream in a wok, bring to the boil and cook over high heat for 2–3 minutes. Add the curry paste and chopped lemon grass and cook, stirring continuously, for 3–4 minutes, or until fragrant.

Reduce the heat to medium, add the stock, coconut milk, soy sauce, palm sugar, lime leaves and lime juice. Cook, stirring, for 3–4 minutes, or until the sugar has dissolved. Stir in the assorted mushrooms and cook for 3–4 minutes, or until tender.

Remove from the heat, stir in the coriander and basil and serve with steamed rice.

Serves 4

Note: For a vegetarian meal, make sure the curry paste you use does not contain shrimp paste.

Tofu with chilli relish and cashews

Chilli relish
80 ml (1/3 cup) peanut oil
12 red Asian shallots, chopped
8 garlic cloves, chopped
8 long red chillies, chopped
2 red capsicums (peppers), chopped
1 tablespoon tamarind concentrate
1 tablespoon soy sauce
100 g (3 1/2 oz) palm sugar, grated

2 tablespoons kecap manis
1 tablespoon peanut oil
6 spring onions (scallions), cut into
  3 cm (1 1/4 inch) lengths
750 g (1 lb 10 oz) silken firm tofu,
  cut into 3 cm (1 1/4 inch) cubes
25 g (3/4 cup) fresh Thai basil
100 g (2/3 cup) roasted salted
  cashews

To make the relish, heat half the oil in a frying pan. Add the Asian shallots and garlic and cook over medium heat for 2 minutes. Transfer to a food processor, add the chilli and capsicum and process until smooth. Heat the remaining oil in the pan, add the shallot mixture and cook over medium heat for 2 minutes. Stir in the tamarind, soy sauce and sugar and cook for 20 minutes.

Place 2–3 tablespoons of the relish with the kecap manis in a bowl and mix. Heat the oil in a wok over high heat and swirl to coat. Add the spring onion, cook for 30 seconds, then remove. Add the tofu and stir-fry for 1 minute, then add the relish and kecap manis mixture. Cook for about 3 minutes, or until the tofu is coated and heated through. Return the spring onion to the wok, add the basil and cashews and cook until the basil has wilted.

Serves 4

Asparagus pie

800 g (1 lb 12 oz) fresh asparagus
20 g (¾ oz) butter
½ teaspoon chopped thyme
1 French shallot, chopped
1 large sheet ready-rolled shortcrust
  pastry
80 ml (⅓ cup) cream
2 tablespoons grated Parmesan
  cheese
1 egg
pinch ground nutmeg
1 egg, extra, lightly beaten

Trim the asparagus spears to 10 cm
(4 inches) and cut thick spears in half
lengthways. Heat the butter in a large
frying pan over medium heat and add
the asparagus, thyme and shallot.
Add a tablespoon of water and
season with salt and pepper. Cook,
stirring, for 3 minutes, or until the
asparagus is tender.

Preheat the oven to 200°C (400°F/
Gas 6) and grease a 21 cm (8½ inch)
fluted, loose-based flan tin. Roll the
pastry out to a 2 mm (⅛ inch) thick
circle with a diameter of about 30 cm
(12 inches). Line the flan tin and trim
the pastry using kitchen scissors,
leaving about 8 cm (3 inches) above
the top of the tin. Arrange half the
asparagus in one direction across
the bottom of the dish. Cover with
the remaining asparagus, running in
the opposite direction.

Combine the cream, Parmesan, egg
and nutmeg and season. Pour over
the asparagus. Fold the pastry over
the filling, forming loose pleats. Brush
with beaten egg and bake in the
centre of the oven for 25 minutes,
or until golden.

Serves 6

Tomato tarte tatin

12 Roma (plum) tomatoes
4 tablespoons olive oil
3 red onions, finely sliced
2 garlic cloves, finely sliced
1 tablespoon balsamic vinegar
1 teaspoon soft brown sugar
15 g (¼ cup) finely shredded basil
60 g (2¼ oz) goat's cheese
1 sheet butter puff pastry

Preheat the oven to 150°C (300°F/ Gas 2). Cut a cross in the base of the tomatoes. Cover with boiling water for 30 seconds, then plunge into cold water. Peel the skin away, then cut the tomatoes in half lengthways, and season well. Place the tomatoes cut-side up on a rack on a baking tray. Cook in the oven for 3 hours.

Heat 2 tablespoons of oil in a heavy-based saucepan, add onions and cook over very low heat, stirring often, for 1 hour or until caramelized.

When the tomatoes are ready, remove from the oven, and increase the oven temperature to 200°C (400°F/Gas 6).

In a 20 cm (8 inch) ovenproof frying pan, heat the remaining olive oil over medium heat. Add the garlic, vinegar, sugar and 1 tablespoon of water, and heat until the sugar dissolves. Remove from the heat. Arrange the tomatoes in concentric circles cut-side up in one layer. Top with the onions, basil and crumbled goat's cheese. Cover with the puff pastry, trim the edges, and tuck the pastry down the side of the pan around the tomatoes. Bake for 25–30 minutes, or until the pastry is golden. Invert the tart onto a plate, cool to room temperature and serve.

Serves 4

Ravioli with roasted red capsicum sauce

6 red capsicums (peppers)
625 g (1 lb 6 oz) ravioli
2 tablespoons olive oil
3 garlic cloves, crushed
2 leeks, thinly sliced
1 tablespoon chopped oregano
2 teaspoons soft brown sugar
250 ml (1 cup) hot vegetable or
   chicken stock

Cut the capsicums into large pieces, removing the seeds and membrane. Cook, skin-side up, under a hot grill (broiler) until the skin blackens and blisters. Cool in a plastic bag, then peel away the skin.

Cook the pasta in a large saucepan of boiling water until *al dente*.

Meanwhile, heat the olive oil in a frying pan and cook the garlic and leek over medium heat for 3–4 minutes, or until softened. Add the oregano and brown sugar and stir for 1 minute.

Place the capsicum and leek mixture in a food processor or blender, season with salt and pepper and process until combined. Add the stock and process until smooth. Drain the pasta and return to the saucepan. Gently toss the sauce through the ravioli over low heat until warmed through. Divide among four serving bowls and serve immediately.

Serves 4

Zucchini omelette

80 g (3 oz) butter
400 g (14 oz) zucchini (courgettes),
   sliced
1 tablespoon finely chopped basil
pinch ground nutmeg
8 eggs, lightly beaten

Melt half the butter in a non-stick 23 cm (9 inch) frying pan. Add the zucchini and cook over medium heat for 8 minutes, or until lightly golden. Stir in the basil and nutmeg, season with salt and pepper and cook for 30 seconds. Transfer to a bowl and keep warm.

Wipe out the pan, return it to the heat and melt the remaining butter. Lightly season the eggs and pour into the pan. Stir gently over high heat. Stop stirring when the mixture begins to set in uniform, fluffy small clumps. Reduce the heat and lift the edges with a fork to prevent it catching. Shake the pan from side to side to prevent the omelette sticking. When it is almost set but still runny on the surface, spread the zucchini down the centre. Using a spatula, fold the omelette over and slide onto a plate. Serve immediately.

Serves 4

Sides

Honey roasted root vegetables

60 g (2¼ oz) butter
2 tablespoons honey
4 thyme sprigs
3 carrots, peeled and cut into chunks
2 parsnips, peeled and cut into chunks
1 medium orange sweet potato, peeled and cut into chunks
1 medium white sweet potato, peeled and cut into chunks
8 small pickling onions, peeled
8 Jerusalem artichokes, peeled
1 garlic head

Preheat the oven to 200°C (400°F/ Gas 6). Melt the butter in a large ovenproof baking dish over medium heat. Add the honey and thyme and stir. Remove from the heat and add the carrot, parsnip, orange and white sweet potato, onions and Jerusalem artichokes. Season well with salt and pepper and toss gently so they are coated with the honey butter.

Trim the base of the garlic and wrap in foil. Add to the baking dish and place in the oven for 1 hour, turning the vegetables occasionally so they caramelize evenly. When cooked, remove the foil from the garlic and pop the cloves from their skin. Add to the other vegetables and serve.

Serves 4

Mushrooms with sticky balsamic syrup

80 ml (⅓ cup) olive oil
750 g (1 lb 10 oz) baby button
  mushrooms
2 large garlic cloves, finely chopped
3 tablespoons soft brown sugar,
  firmly packed
60 ml (¼ cup) balsamic vinegar
3 teaspoons thyme leaves

Heat the oil in a large, heavy-based, non-stick frying pan. Add the button mushrooms and cook over high heat for 5 minutes, or until slightly softened and golden. Season the mushrooms with salt while they are cooking.

Add the garlic and cook for 1 minute. Stir in the brown sugar, vinegar and 1 tablespoon of water, and boil for 5 minutes, or until reduced by one-third. Season to taste with pepper.

Arrange the mushrooms on a serving plate. Reduce the remaining liquid for 1 minute, or until thick and syrupy. Pour over the mushrooms and garnish with the thyme.

Serves 4

Carrots with coconut, ginger and chilli

1 kg (2 lb 4 oz) carrots, peeled
   and cut into thick batons
60 g (2¼ oz) creamed coconut
   (in a block)
1 garlic clove, crushed
2 teaspoons grated fresh ginger
2 green chillies, seeded and
   chopped
1 teaspoon ground coriander
1 teaspoon ground cumin
1 teaspoon soy sauce
1 teaspoon chopped lime zest
1 tablespoon lime juice
1 teaspoon palm sugar
3 tablespoons peanut oil
2 tablespoons chopped coriander
   (cilantro) leaves
lime wedges, to serve

Preheat the oven to 200°C (400°F/ Gas 6). Bring a large saucepan of water to the boil, blanch the carrots for 5 minutes, then drain well.

Grate the creamed coconut and mix with 2–3 tablespoons of hot water to form a paste. Stir in the garlic, ginger, chilli, coriander, cumin, soy sauce, lime zest, lime juice and palm sugar. Add the carrots and toss to combine.

Pour the peanut oil into a large, shallow-sided roasting tin and heat in the oven for 5 minutes. Toss the carrots in the hot oil, then roast in the oven for 5 minutes. Reduce the heat to 180°C (350°F/Gas 4) and roast for another 20 minutes, or until crisp and golden. Sprinkle with the coriander leaves and serve with lime wedges.

Serves 6

Baked onions stuffed with goat's cheese and sun-dried tomatoes

6 large onions
60 ml (¼ cup) extra virgin olive oil
1 garlic clove, crushed
100 g (3½ oz) sun-dried tomatoes, finely chopped
25 g (⅓ cup) fresh white breadcrumbs
1 tablespoon chopped parsley
2 teaspoons chopped thyme
100 g (3½ oz) mild soft goat's cheese, crumbled
80 g (3 oz) Parmesan cheese, grated
1 egg
250 ml (1 cup) vegetable or chicken stock
1 tablespoon butter

Preheat the oven to 180°C (350°F/Gas 4). Peel the onions, cut a slice off the top and reserve. Using a teaspoon scrape out a cavity almost to the base of the onion, leaving a hole to stuff.

Blanch the onions in a large saucepan of boiling water for 5 minutes, then drain. Heat 2 tablespoons of oil in a small frying pan and cook the garlic for 3 minutes, or until soft. Add the tomato, breadcrumbs and herbs and cook for 1 minute. Remove from the heat and add the goat's cheese and Parmesan. Season and stir in the egg.

Stuff the mixture into each onion cavity. Arrange the onions in a large ovenproof ceramic dish. Pour the stock around the onions and drizzle with the remaining oil. Cover with foil and bake for 45 minutes, basting from time to time. Remove the foil for the last 10 minutes of cooking.

Remove the onions to a serving plate and, over medium heat, simmer the remaining stock for 5–8 minutes, or until reduced by half and syrupy. Reduce the heat and whisk in the butter. The sauce should be smooth and glossy. Season to taste and spoon over the onions.

Serves 6

Snake beans stir-fried with Thai basil, garlic and chilli

3 tablespoons soy sauce
60 ml (¼ cup) vegetable or chicken
   stock
2 tablespoons vegetable oil
1 teaspoon red curry paste
1 red Asian shallot, finely chopped
3 garlic cloves, finely sliced
1 small red chilli, seeds removed
   and sliced
500 g (1 lb 2 oz) snake beans,
   cut into 8 cm (3 inch) lengths
   on the diagonal
20 g (⅓ cup) Thai basil leaves

Combine the soy sauce, stock and
60 ml (¼ cup) water and set aside.

Heat a wok over high heat, add the
vegetable oil, red curry paste, shallot,
garlic and chilli and stir-fry until
fragrant. Add the snake beans and
cook for 5 minutes. Stir in the sauce
and cook, tossing gently, until the
beans are tender. Remove from the
heat and season well. Stir in half the
basil and scatter the rest on top as
a garnish. Serve immediately.

Serves 4

Rosemary and garlic roasted potatoes

1.5 kg (3 lb 5 oz) potatoes, peeled
  and cut into large chunks
80 ml (⅓ cup) olive oil
12 garlic cloves in the skin,
  root end trimmed
2 tablespoons rosemary leaves

Preheat the oven to 200°C (400°F/ Gas 6). Cook the potatoes in a large saucepan of boiling salted water for 10 minutes, or until just tender. Drain in a colander, and sit for 5 minutes so they dry slightly.

Meanwhile, pour the olive oil into a large roasting tray, and heat in the oven for 5 minutes. Add the potatoes to the tray (they should sizzle in the hot oil), add the garlic and rosemary and season liberally with salt and pepper. Roast, stirring occasionally, so they cook evenly, for about 1 hour, or until golden and crisp. Serve with the roasted garlic cloves popped from their skin and the rosemary leaves.

Serves 4–6

Pepperonata

3 red capsicums (peppers)
3 yellow capsicums (peppers)
2 tablespoons olive oil
1 large red onion, thinly sliced
3 large fresh tomatoes, finely
    chopped
1 tablespoon sugar
2 tablespoons balsamic vinegar
2 garlic cloves, finely chopped
5 g (¼ cup) flat-leaf (Italian) parsley,
    chopped

Slice the red and yellow capsicums into 2 cm (¾ inch) wide strips. Heat the oil in a large heavy-based frying pan and cook the onion over low heat for 5 minutes, or until softened. Add the capsicum strips and cook for another 5 minutes. Add the tomatoes and cook, covered, over low–medium heat for 10 minutes, or until the vegetables are soft. Remove the lid and simmer for an extra 2 minutes.

Stir in the sugar and vinegar. Place in a serving bowl and scatter with the garlic and parsley. Season with salt and freshly ground black pepper.

Serves 4

Baked sweet potato with saffron and pine nut butter

1 kg (2 lb 4 oz) white sweet potatoes
2 tablespoons vegetable oil
1 tablespoon milk
pinch saffron threads
100 g (3½ oz) unsalted butter,
   softened
40 g (¼ cup) pine nuts, toasted
2 tablespoons finely chopped
   parsley
2 garlic cloves, crushed

Preheat the oven to 180°C (350°F/ Gas 4). Peel the sweet potatoes and chop into large chunks. Toss to coat with oil. Place them on a baking tray, cover with foil and roast for 20 minutes.

Warm the milk, add the saffron and leave to infuse for 5 minutes. Put the butter, milk mixture, pine nuts, parsley and garlic in a food processor and pulse to combine. Take care not to overprocess, the nuts should still have some texture. Place a sheet of plastic wrap on the workbench, put the butter in the centre and roll up to form a neat log, about 4 cm (1½ inches) in diameter. Refrigerate the butter for half an hour.

Remove the foil from the potatoes and roast, uncovered, for another 30 minutes, or until they are cooked through (test this by piercing with a skewer). Bring the butter to room temperature, unwrap, cut into 1 cm (½ inch) slices and return to the refrigerator to keep cool.

Arrange the butter slices over the sweet potato, season with salt and ground black pepper and serve.

Serves 4–6

Chargrilled eggplant with fresh lemon pesto

2 large eggplants (aubergines),
    cut into 1.5 cm (⅝ inch) slices
    or 8 small eggplants (aubergines),
    halved lengthways
160 ml (⅔ cup) extra virgin olive oil
60 g (2 cups) basil leaves
20 g (1 cup) parsley
50 g (⅓ cup) pine nuts, toasted
1½ garlic cloves
60 g (2¼ oz) grated Parmesan
    cheese
grated zest of 1 lemon
60 ml (¼ cup) lemon juice

Brush both sides of the eggplant slices with 2 tablespoons of extra virgin olive oil. Heat a chargrill pan (griddle) until hot, and cook the eggplant slices for 3 minutes, or until golden and cooked through on both sides. If you are using baby eggplant, grill only on the cut side, and finish off in a 200°C (400°F/Gas 6) oven for 5–8 minutes, or until soft. Cover the eggplant to keep warm.

Place the basil, parsley, pine nuts, garlic, Parmesan, lemon zest and lemon juice in a food processor, and blend together. Slowly add the remaining olive oil and process until the mixture forms a smooth paste. Season with salt and freshly ground black pepper.

Stack the eggplant on a platter, drizzling some pesto between each layer. Serve immediately.

Serves 4–6

Braised red cabbage

60 g (2¼ oz) butter
1 onion, chopped
2 garlic cloves, crushed
900 g (2 lb) red cabbage, sliced
2 green apples, peeled, cored
  and diced
4 cloves
¼ teaspoon nutmeg
1 fresh bay leaf
2 juniper berries
1 cinnamon stick
80 ml (⅓ cup) red wine
50 ml (2½ tablespoons) red wine
  vinegar
2 tablespoons soft brown sugar
1 tablespoon redcurrant jelly
500 ml (2 cups) vegetable or
  chicken stock

Preheat the oven to 150°C (300°F/ Gas 2). Heat 40 g (1½ oz) of butter in a large casserole dish, add the onion and garlic and cook over medium heat for 5 minutes. Add the cabbage and cook for another 10 minutes, stirring frequently.

Add the apples, cloves, nutmeg, bay leaf, juniper berries and cinnamon stick to the dish. Pour in the red wine and cook for 5 minutes, then add the red wine vinegar, brown sugar, redcurrant jelly and stock. Bring to the boil, then cover and cook in the oven for 2 hours.

After 2 hours of cooking check the liquid level — there should be only about 125 ml (½ cup) left. Stir in the remaining butter, season well with salt and pepper, and serve.

Serves 4–6

Zucchini with mint and feta

6 zucchini (courgettes)
1 tablespoon olive oil
70 g (2½ oz) feta cheese,
   crumbled
1 teaspoon finely grated
   lemon zest
½ teaspoon chopped garlic
1 tablespoon lemon juice
1 tablespoon extra virgin olive oil
2 tablespoons shredded mint
2 tablespoons shredded parsley

Slice each zucchini lengthways into four thick batons. Heat the olive oil in a heavy-based, non-stick frying pan and cook the zucchini over medium heat for 3–4 minutes, or until just tender and lightly golden. Arrange on a serving plate.

Crumble the feta over the zucchini. Mix the lemon zest, garlic and lemon juice in a small jug. Whisk in the extra virgin olive oil with a fork until well combined, then pour the dressing over the zucchini. Top with the mint and parsley, and season with salt and pepper. Serve warm.

Serves 4

Jerusalem artichokes roasted with red wine and garlic

800 g (1 lb 12 oz) Jerusalem
    artichokes
1 tablespoon lemon juice
2 tablespoons red wine
2 tablespoons olive oil
1 tablespoon tamari
2 garlic cloves, crushed
dash Tabasco sauce
2 tablespoons vegetable stock
2 tablespoons chopped parsley

Preheat the oven to 200°C (400°F/ Gas 6). Scrub the artichokes well, then cut them in half lengthways, and place in a bowl of water mixed with the lemon juice.

Combine the red wine, olive oil, tamari, garlic, Tabasco sauce and stock in a baking tray. Drain and quickly dry the artichoke halves with paper towels. Place in the baking tray, and toss all the ingredients together. Season with salt and freshly ground black pepper.

Bake, covered, for 40 minutes, or until tender, then uncover and bake for another 5 minutes, or until the juices have formed a reduced glaze. Remove from the oven, and toss with the parsley before serving.

Serves 4

Potatoes in parchment

700 g (1 lb 9 oz) baby potatoes,
halved
30 g (1 oz) butter, cut into small
cubes
1 tablespoon thyme sprigs
6 garlic cloves, unpeeled
2 tablespoons olive oil
sea salt, to serve

Preheat the oven to 200°C (400°F/ Gas 6). Cut two pieces of baking paper, each 50 cm (20 inches) long. Place half of the potatoes in a single layer on one piece of paper, scatter with half of the butter, half of the thyme and 3 cloves of garlic. Drizzle with 1 tablespoon of olive oil. Bring the long edges of the paper together and fold over twice. Fold over the short edges so that the potatoes are sealed within the paper, and place the parcels on a baking tray with the fold side facing down.

Repeat with the remaining ingredients to form a second potato parcel. Bake for 1 hour and 10 minutes, or until the potatoes are tender (test by piercing with a skewer). Serve sprinkled with sea salt.

Serves 4

Creamed spinach

1.5 kg (3 lb 5 oz) English spinach
2 teaspoons butter
1 garlic clove, crushed
1/4 teaspoon freshly grated nutmeg
80 ml (1/3 cup) thick (double/heavy)
  cream
1 tablespoon grated Parmesan
  cheese

Remove the tough ends from the spinach stalks and wash the leaves well. Shake to remove any excess water from the leaves, but do not dry completely.

Melt the butter in a large frying pan. Add the crushed garlic and the spinach, season with nutmeg, salt and pepper, and cook over medium heat until the spinach is just wilted. Remove from the heat and place the spinach in a sieve. Press down well to squeeze out all of the excess moisture. Transfer to a chopping board and, using a mezzaluna or a sharp knife, chop the spinach finely.

Pour the cream into the frying pan and heat gently. Add the spinach to the pan and stir until warmed through. Arrange the spinach on a serving dish and sprinkle with the Parmesan.

Serves 4–6

Roasted beetroot with horseradish cream

8 beetroot
2 tablespoons olive oil
2 teaspoons honey
1½ tablespoons creamed
  horseradish
100 g (3½ oz) sour cream
chopped parsley, to garnish

Preheat the oven to 200°C (400°F/ Gas 6). Scrub and peel the beetroot, trim the ends and cut into quarters. Place the oil and honey in a small bowl and mix well. Season with salt and freshly ground black pepper.

Place the beetroot on a large square of foil and drizzle with the honey mixture, coating them well. Enclose the beetroot loosely in the foil. Bake for 1 hour, or until the beetroot are tender when pierced with a skewer.

Meanwhile, combine the horseradish and sour cream, and season lightly. Once the beetroot are cooked, remove from the oven and leave in the foil for 5 minutes. Remove from the foil and serve with a generous dollop of the horseradish cream and the parsley garnish.

Serves 4

Deep-fried Parmesan carrots

500 g (1 lb 2 oz) baby (dutch)
   carrots
60 g (½ cup) plain (all-purpose)
   flour
2 teaspoons ground cumin
2 eggs
250 g (3 cups) fine fresh white
   breadcrumbs
1 tablespoon chopped parsley
65 g (⅔ cup) finely grated
   Parmesan cheese
oil, for deep-frying

Trim the leafy carrot tops, leaving about 2 cm (¾ inch), and wash the carrots. Bring a large saucepan of water to the boil, add 1 teaspoon of salt and cook the carrots for 5 minutes, or until tender (test with a metal skewer). Drain, dry well with paper towels and leave to cool.

Sift the flour and cumin onto a sheet of greaseproof paper, then beat the eggs together in a wide, shallow bowl. Combine the breadcrumbs, parsley and Parmesan, and season with salt and pepper. Roll the carrots in the flour, then the eggs and finally the breadcrumbs. For an extra crispy coating repeat this process.

Fill a deep, heavy-based saucepan one-third full of oil and heat until a cube of bread dropped into the oil browns in 20 seconds. Deep-fry the carrots in batches until golden and crisp. Serve immediately.

Serves 6

Green beans with feta and tomatoes

1 tablespoon olive oil
1 onion, chopped
2 garlic cloves, crushed
1½ tablespoons chopped oregano
125 ml (½ cup) white wine
425 g (15 oz) tin diced tomatoes
250 g (9 oz) green beans, trimmed
1 tablespoon balsamic vinegar
200 g (7 oz) feta cheese, cut into
  1.5 cm (⁵/₈ inch) cubes

Heat the oil in a saucepan, add the onion and cook over medium heat for 3–5 minutes, or until soft. Add the garlic and half the oregano, and cook for another minute. Pour in the white wine and cook for 3 minutes, or until reduced by one-third.

Stir in the diced tomato and cook, uncovered, for 10 minutes. Add the beans and cook, covered, for another 10 minutes.

Stir in the balsamic vinegar, feta and remaining oregano. Season with salt and pepper, and serve.

Serves 4

Orange sweet potato wedges with tangy cumin mayonnaise

2½ tablespoons olive oil
1 kg (2 lb 4 oz) orange sweet
  potato, peeled and cut into
  6 cm (2½ inch) long wedges
200 g (7 oz) mayonnaise
60 ml (¼ cup) lime juice
1 teaspoon honey
1 heaped tablespoon roughly
  chopped coriander (cilantro)
1½ teaspoons ground cumin

Preheat the oven to 200°C (400°F/ Gas 6). Place the olive oil in a large roasting tin and heat in the oven for 5 minutes.

Place the sweet potato in the tin in a single layer, season with salt and pepper and bake for 35 minutes, turning occasionally.

While the sweet potato is cooking, place the mayonnaise, lime juice, honey, coriander and cumin in a food processor, and blend until smooth.

Drain the wedges on crumpled paper towels and serve with the tangy cumin mayonnaise on the side.

Serves 4

Cauliflower pilaf

200 g (1 cup) basmati rice
2 tablespoons olive oil
1 large onion, thinly sliced
1/4 teaspoon cardamom seeds
1/2 teaspoon ground turmeric
1 cinnamon stick
1 teaspoon cumin seeds
1/4 teaspoon cayenne pepper
500 ml (2 cups) vegetable or
    chicken stock
800 g (1 lb 12 oz) head cauliflower,
    trimmed and cut into florets
20 g (1/3 cup) chopped coriander
    (cilantro) leaves

Put the rice in a sieve and rinse under cold running water. Set aside to drain.

Heat the oil in a saucepan that has a tightly fitting lid. Cook the onion over medium heat, stirring frequently, for 5 minutes, or until soft and lightly golden. Add the spices and cook, stirring, for 1 minute.

Add the rice to the pan and stir to coat in the spices. Add the stock and cauliflower, stirring to combine.

Cover with the lid and bring to the boil. Reduce the heat to very low and cook for 15 minutes, or until the rice and cauliflower are tender and all the stock has been absorbed.

Fold the coriander through the rice, and serve immediately.

Serves 6

Fennel with walnut parsley crust

2 tablespoons lemon juice
9 small fennel bulbs, halved
  lengthways
1 teaspoon fennel seeds
100 g (1 cup) grated Parmesan
  cheese
160 g (2 cups) fresh breadcrumbs
100 g (3½ oz) chopped walnuts
1 tablespoon chopped parsley
2 teaspoons lemon zest
2 garlic cloves, chopped
250 ml (1 cup) vegetable or
  chicken stock
2¼ tablespoons butter

Bring a large saucepan of water to the boil and add the lemon juice and 1 teaspoon of salt. Cook the fennel in the acidulated water for 5–10 minutes, or until tender, then drain and cool.

Heat a dry frying pan and roast the fennel seeds over medium heat for 1 minute to release their flavour. Tip the seeds into a food processor, add the Parmesan, breadcrumbs, walnuts, parsley, lemon zest and garlic, and pulse gently to combine. Stir in 2 tablespoons of stock to moisten the mixture.

Place the fennel, flat-side up, in an ovenproof ceramic dish and spoon on the stuffing, spreading to completely cover each piece. Pour the remaining stock around the fennel and top each piece with ½ teaspoon of butter. Bake for 25 minutes, basting from time to time, until the top is golden and the fennel is cooked through. Serve drizzled with the braising juices.

Serves 4

Potato rösti

750 g (1 lb 10 oz) waxy potatoes,
  peeled
1 small onion, finely sliced
2 tablespoons chopped parsley
30 g (1 oz) butter
2 teaspoons olive oil

Boil the potatoes for 10–15 minutes, or until they just begin to soften. Drain, and allow to cool. Grate the potatoes and place in a large bowl with the onion and parsley, and season well with salt and pepper.

Heat the butter and oil in a non-stick frying pan over medium–low heat. When the butter has melted, add the potato mixture to the pan, spreading the mixture out, but not pressing too firmly. Cover the pan and cook for 8–10 minutes, or until golden and crispy. Halfway through the cooking time, check to ensure the rösti is not burning. Carefully turn by flipping the whole rösti onto a plate then sliding it, uncooked-side down, back into the pan. Cover and cook for 5 minutes, or until golden brown. Cut into four pieces and serve.

Serves 4

Cabbage with leek and mustard seeds

1 tablespoon oil
2 tablespoons unsalted butter
2 teaspoons black mustard seeds
2 leeks, washed and thinly sliced
500 g (1 lb 2 oz) thinly shredded
  cabbage
1 tablespoon lemon juice
5 tablespoons crème fraîche
2 tablespoons chopped parsley

Heat the oil and butter together, add the mustard seeds, and cook until they start to pop. Add the leeks and cook gently for 5–8 minutes, or until softened. Stir in the cabbage and cook over low heat for 4 minutes, or until it wilts and softens.

Season the cabbage well with salt and pepper. Add the lemon juice and crème fraîche, and cook for 1 minute longer. Stir in the chopped parsley and serve immediately.

Serves 4–6

Roasted red onion and Roma tomatoes with balsamic vinaigrette

oil, to brush
8 Roma (plum) tomatoes
2 red onions
2 garlic cloves
1½ tablespoons balsamic vinegar
1 teaspoon French mustard
60 ml (¼ cup) extra virgin olive oil

Preheat the oven to 150°C (300°F/ Gas 2) and lightly brush a baking tray with oil.

Cut the tomatoes into quarters and arrange on the tray. Remove the tops of the onion and peel. Cut each onion into 8 wedges and place on the tray with the tomatoes. Place the garlic in the middle of the tray, spaced 5 cm (2 inches) apart and season all of the vegetables well. Roast for 1 hour.

Arrange the tomatoes and onions on a serving plate. Peel the garlic and crush in a small bowl. Add the balsamic vinegar and mustard to the garlic and, using a small wire whisk, beat in the olive oil, adding it slowly in a thin stream. Season the dressing well and drizzle over the onions and tomatoes. Serve immediately.

Serves 4

Parsnip chips

4 parsnips
oil, for deep-frying
1/4 teaspoon ground cumin

Trim and peel the parsnips. Using a vegetable peeler, cut them into long, thick strips.

Fill a deep, heavy-based saucepan one-third full of oil and heat until a cube of bread dropped in the oil browns in 15 seconds. Deep-fry the parsnip strips in batches for 1 minute, or until they are golden and crisp. Remove from the oil and drain on crumpled paper towels.

Mix 2 teaspoons of salt with the cumin in a small bowl. Put the hot parsnip chips in a large bowl and season with the cumin mixture. Serve immediately.

Serves 4

Gai larn with ginger, lime and peanuts

600 g (1 lb 5 oz) gai larn (Chinese broccoli)
40 g (1 1/2 oz) tamarind pulp
1 small red chilli
1 tablespoon peanut oil
2 garlic cloves, finely chopped
3 teaspoons finely grated fresh ginger
1 tablespoon sugar
1 tablespoon lime juice
1 teaspoon sesame oil
1 tablespoon roasted unsalted peanuts, finely chopped

Trim the ends from the gai larn and slice in half. Place the tamarind in a bowl and pour in 60 ml (1/4 cup) boiling water. Allow to steep for 5 minutes, then strain, discarding the solids.

Slice the chilli in half, remove the seeds and membrane and chop finely. Heat a wok until very hot, add the peanut oil and swirl it around to coat the wok. Add the gai larn and stir-fry for 2–3 minutes, or until wilted. Add the chilli, garlic and ginger, and cook for another minute. Add the sugar, lime juice and 1 tablespoon of tamarind liquid and simmer for 1 minute.

Remove the gai larn to a serving plate and drizzle with the sesame oil. Scatter with peanuts and season to taste with salt and pepper.

Serves 4

Brussels sprouts with chestnut and sage butter

25 g (1 oz) butter, softened
25 g (1 oz) peeled, cooked chestnuts, finely chopped (see Note)
1 teaspoon chopped sage
700 g (1 lb 9 oz) Brussels sprouts, trimmed

Put the butter, chopped chestnuts and sage in a bowl and mix together well. Scrape onto a large piece of greaseproof paper and shape into a log, using the paper to help shape the butter. Wrap in the paper and refrigerate until firm.

Cook the Brussels sprouts in salted, boiling water for 10–12 minutes, or until tender. Drain well. Take care not to overcook the sprouts or they will become soggy. Cut the chilled chestnut butter into thin slices. Toss four of the slices with the sprouts until they are evenly coated in butter, and season well. Arrange the remaining slices on top of the sprouts and serve immediately.

Serves 4

Note: If chestnuts are unavailable, use toasted walnuts.

Tagliatelle of root vegetables in spiced cream

4 large carrots
2 large parsnips
iced water
185 ml (¾ cup) cream
1 garlic clove, crushed
35 g (⅓ cup) finely grated
  Parmesan cheese
2 tablespoons chopped
  chives

Peel the outer skin from the carrots and parsnips, and discard. Peel long thin strips from the vegetables until you reach the hard core. Bring a large saucepan of water to the boil, add 1 teaspoon of salt and blanch the vegetables for 1 minute. Drain, then refresh in a bowl of iced water.

Pour the cream into a saucepan and add the crushed garlic. Stir over medium heat until reduced to about 100 ml (3½ fl oz). Add 2 tablespoons Parmesan and 1 tablespoon chives, and season well with salt and freshly ground black pepper.

Drain the vegetables, then add to the cream and stir gently over medium heat for 2 minutes, or until warmed through. Garnish with the remaining Parmesan and chives, and serve.

Serves 4

Mashed carrots with cumin seeds

6 carrots
1 tablespoon olive oil
2 garlic cloves, finely chopped
1 teaspoon ground turmeric
2 teaspoons finely grated fresh
  ginger
60 g (¼ cup) thick Greek-style
  yoghurt
2 teaspoons prepared harissa
2 tablespoons chopped coriander
  (cilantro) leaves
2 teaspoons lime juice
1 teaspoon cumin seeds

Peel the carrots and cut into 2.5 cm (1 inch) chunks. Place them in a large saucepan and cover with cold water. Bring to the boil, then reduce the heat and simmer for 3 minutes. Drain and allow to dry.

Heat the olive oil in a heavy-based, non-stick saucepan. Cook the garlic, ground turmeric and ginger over medium heat for 1 minute, or until fragrant. Add the carrots, and cook for 3 minutes. Stir in 1 tablespoon water and cook, covered, over low heat for 10–15 minutes, or until the carrots are soft. Transfer the mixture to a bowl and roughly mash.

Add the yoghurt, harissa, coriander and lime juice to the carrots and stir to combine. Season to taste with salt and freshly ground black pepper.

Heat a heavy-based frying pan, add the cumin seeds, and dry-fry for 1–2 minutes, or until fragrant. Scatter over the mashed carrots and serve.

Serves 4

Indian-style spinach

2 tablespoons ghee or vegetable oil
1 onion, thinly sliced
2 garlic cloves, finely chopped
2 teaspoons finely grated fresh ginger
1 teaspoon brown mustard seeds
1/2 teaspoon ground cumin
1/4 teaspoon ground coriander
1 teaspoon ground turmeric
1/2 teaspoon garam masala
350 g (12 oz) English spinach,
   trimmed
60 ml (1/4 cup) cream
1 tablespoon lemon juice

Heat a wok until very hot. Add the ghee and swirl it around to coat the wok. Stir-fry the onion over medium heat for 2 minutes to soften. Add the garlic, ginger, brown mustard seeds, cumin, coriander, turmeric and garam masala, and cook for 1 minute, or until fragrant.

Roughly tear the spinach leaves in half and add to the spice mixture. Cook for 1–2 minutes, or until wilted. Add the cream, simmer for 2 minutes, then add the lemon juice and season with salt and freshly ground black pepper. Serve hot.

Serves 4

Pumpkin with chilli

800 g (1 lb 12 oz) butternut
  pumpkin (squash)
2 tablespoons oil
2 garlic cloves, crushed
1 teaspoon grated fresh ginger
2 bird's eye chillies, finely chopped
1 teaspoon finely grated lime zest
1 tablespoon lime juice
1½ tablespoons light soy sauce
185 ml (¾ cup) vegetable or
  chicken stock
1 tablespoon soy sauce
1 teaspoon shaved palm sugar
35 g (¾ cup) coriander (cilantro)
  leaves, chopped

Peel the pumpkin, and scoop out the seeds to give about 600 g (1 lb 5 oz) of flesh. Cut the flesh into 1.5 cm (⅝ inch) cubes.

Heat the oil in a large frying pan or wok over medium heat, add the garlic, ginger and chilli, and stir-fry for 1 minute. Keep moving the garlic and chilli around the pan to ensure they don't burn, as this will make them taste bitter. Add the pumpkin, lime zest, lime juice, light soy sauce, stock, soy sauce and palm sugar, then cover and cook for 10 minutes or until the pumpkin is tender.

Remove the lid and gently stir for 5 minutes, or until any remaining liquid has reduced. Gently stir in the chopped coriander and serve immediately.

Serves 4

Fried green tomatoes with a cornmeal crust

750 g (1 lb 10 oz) unripe, green
  tomatoes
60 g (½ cup) plain (all-purpose) flour
225 g (1½ cups) yellow cornmeal
2 teaspoons finely chopped thyme
2 teaspoons finely chopped marjoram
50 g (½ cup) grated Parmesan
  cheese
2 eggs, beaten with 1 tablespoon
  water
olive oil, for pan-frying

Preheat the oven to 180°C (350°F/ Gas 4). Cut the tomatoes into 1 cm (½ inch) slices and season with salt. Season the flour well with salt and freshly ground black pepper and place in a shallow bowl. Combine the cornmeal, thyme, marjoram and Parmesan. Dip the tomato slices in the flour, coating all surfaces. Next dip in the beaten egg, followed by the cornmeal mixture. Set the tomatoes aside in a single layer.

Fill a large, heavy-based frying pan with olive oil to 5 mm (¼ inch) deep. Heat over medium heat until a cube of bread dropped in the oil browns in 20 seconds. Reduce the heat a little, then cook the tomato slices in batches for 2–3 minutes each side, or until golden. Remove with tongs and drain on paper towels. Transfer the tomato slices to a plate and keep them warm in the oven while the rest are being cooked. Add more oil to the pan as necessary to maintain the level. Serve hot.

Serves 4–6

Sides

Sweet corn with lime and chilli butter

4 corn cobs
50 g (1¾ oz) butter
2 tablespoons olive oil
1 stem lemon grass, bruised
   and cut in half
3 small bird's eye chillies, seeded
   and finely chopped
2 tablespoons lime zest, finely
   grated
2 tablespoons lime juice
2 tablespoons finely chopped
   coriander (cilantro) leaves

Remove the skins and silky threads from the corn cobs. Wash well, then using a long sharp knife cut each cob into 2 cm (¾ inch) chunks.

Heat the butter and oil in a large saucepan over low heat. Add the lemon grass and braise gently for 5 minutes, then remove from the pan. Add the chilli and cook for 2 minutes. Stir in the grated lime zest, lime juice, 3 tablespoons of water and the corn. Cover and cook, shaking the pan frequently, for 5–8 minutes, or until the corn is tender. Season well, then stir in the coriander and serve hot.

Serves 4

Note: Offer plenty of napkins with this dish, as the corn chunks are quite messy to eat.

Index

Index

Index

Index

Published by Murdoch Books Pty Limited

Editorial Director: Diana Hill
Editor: Rachel Carter
Creative Director: Marylouise Brammer Designer: Michelle Cutler
Photographers: Jared Fowler, Ian Hofstetter Stylists: Jane Collins, Cherise Koch
Food preparation: Michelle Earl, Joanne Kelly
Production: Monika Paratore

Chief Executive: Juliet Rogers
Publisher: Kay Scarlett

National Library of Australia Cataloguing-in-Publication Data: Vegie food. Includes index.
ISBN 1 74045 305 0. 1. Vegetarian cookery. I. Fowler, Jared. II. Koch, Cherise.
641.5636

Printed by Sing Cheong Printing Co. Ltd
PRINTED IN HONG KONG
First printed 2004. Reprinted 2004, 2005 (twice).

You may find cooking times vary depending on the oven you are using. For fan-forced ovens,
as a general rule, set the oven temperature to 20°C lower than indicated in the recipe.
We have used 20 ml tablespoon measures. If you are using a 15 ml tablespoon, for most recipes
the difference will not be noticeable. However, for recipes using small amounts of flour and cornflour,
add an extra teaspoon for each tablespoon specified. We have used 60 g (Grade 3) eggs in all recipes.

IMPORTANT: Those who might be at risk from the effects of salmonella poisoning (the elderly, pregnant
women, young children and those suffering from immune deficiency diseases) should consult their GP
with any concerns about eating raw eggs.

Published by:
AUSTRALIA
Murdoch Books Pty Ltd
Pier 8/9, 23 Hickson Rd
Millers Point NSW 2000
Phone: + 61 (0) 2 8220 2000
Fax: + 61 (0) 2 8220 2558

UK
Murdoch Books UK Ltd
Erico House, 6th Floor North
93–99 Upper Richmond Rd
Putney, London SW15 2TG
Phone: +44 (0) 20 8785 5995
Fax: +44 (0) 20 8785 5985